The Russian Mafia in America

ILLUSTRATED

RUSSIAN ORGANIZED CRIME IN THE UNITED STATES

HEARING BEFORE THE PERMANENT SUBCOMMITTEE ON INVESTIGATIONS OF THE COMMITTEE ON GOVERNMENTAL AFFAIRS UNITED STATES SENATE

ONE HUNDRED FOURTH CONGRESS SECOND SESSION

MAY 15, 1996

2

RUSSIAN ORGANIZED CRIME IN THE UNITED STATES
WEDNESDAY, MAY 15, 1996

U.S. Senate,
Permanent Subcommittee on Investigations,
OF THE Committee on Governmental Affairs,
Washington, DC.
The Subcommittee met, pursuant to notice, at 9:40 a.m., in room
SD-342, Dirksen Senate Office Building, Hon. William V. ROTH, Jr.,
Chairman of the Subcommittee, presiding.
Present: Senators ROTH, Cohen, Nunn, Lieberman and Dorgan.

OPENING STATEMENT OF SENATOR ROTH

Senator William Roth.

Senator ROTH. The Subcommittee will please come to order.

This morning, the Permanent Subcommittee on Investigations continues to fulfill its mandate of presenting to Congress and to the American people the changing face of organized crime in the United States. Today we will examine the currently emerging threat posed by Russian organized crime here in America.

Over its long history, this Subcommittee has been at the forefront of exposing the dangers posed by organized crime groups operating within our borders, including Colombian and Asian criminal organizations. We found that the spotlight of exposure and the glare of public scrutiny are among our most effective weapons against these resourceful and resilient groups, which operate most effectively in the netherworld of secrecy, fear and intimidation. We can be particularly effective if we can expose an organized group in its early stages, and that is why we are here today.

Through experience, we know how hard it is to dislodge any criminal group once it has become entrenched in legitimate businesses and its members assimilated into American communities. It may be useful to begin with a short geography lesson. When we used the term "Russian organized crime" in the course of this hearing, we are referring to organized crime from all the republics of the former Soviet Union, not only from the Republic of Russia.

Whacked by the Russian Mobs

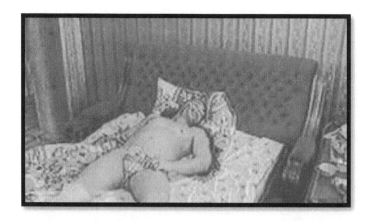

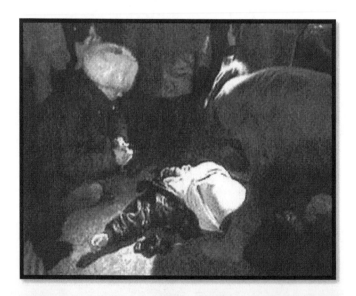

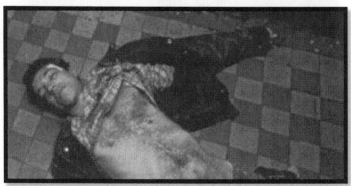

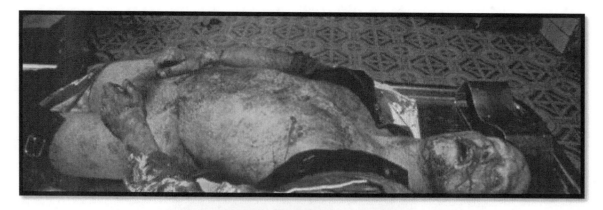

We realize the limitations of this definition but have chosen to use this phrase because of its widespread recognition and acceptance.

I also want to make clear that the vast majority of former Soviet citizens currently residing in America are law-abiding, hard-working and extremely productive members of our society. In fact, these are the people who are most often the victims of this criminal activity. Like most other international organized crime groups, those from the former Soviet Union start out by preying primarily on their own ethnic communities in the United States.

The fact that former Soviet émigrés to this country suffer disproportionately at the hands of criminals who are their former countrymen leads, unfortunately, to an often unspoken but nevertheless widely held point of view, namely, that because former Soviet citizens are most often the victims of these crimes, the rest of us need not concern ourselves with this problem. I categorically reject that view. First, all residents of our Nation are entitled to protection no matter what their backgrounds.

Moscow Boos with his bodyguard

Second, if we have learned anything from our previous investigations, it is that all organized criminals, whatever their ethnic origin, eventually extend their greedy tentacles beyond their native communities into American society as a whole in a never-ending reach for more money, power and influence.

Russian organized crime presents a textbook example of what I have referred to as "the new international criminals"; they are a breed set apart from traditional organized crime. Despite having roots that can be traced back to earlier times, criminals from the former Soviet Union have thrived by adapting to and exploiting modern technology. They have created global communication networks through the use of satellite telephones, cellular clone phones and encrypted fax machines.

Semyon Mogilevich. Semion Yudkovich Mogilevich (Born June 30, 1946) is a Ukrainian-born organized crime boss, believed by European and United States federal law enforcement agencies to be the "boss of bosses" of most Russian Mafia syndicates in the world. Mogilevich's nicknames include "Don Semyon", and "The Brainy Don" (because of his business acumen). He is believed to direct a vast criminal empire and is described by the FBI as "the most dangerous mobster in the world". He is said to control RosUkrEnergo, a company currently actively involved in Russia–Ukraine gas disputes. Secret US diplomatic cables, released by Wikileaks, describe Mogilevich as the figure in charge of both RosUkrEnergo and Raiffeisen Bank. They also state that Mogilevich has close links to Gazprom, the Russian state energy company. He is based in Moscow, Russia. He is most closely associated with the Solntsevskaya Bratva crime group. Political figures he has close alliances with include Yury Luzhkov, the former Mayor of Moscow, Dmytro Firtash and Leonid Derkach, former head of the Security Service of Ukraine. Oleksandr Turchynov, former Prime Minister of the Ukraine, went to court for allegedly destroying files pertaining to Mogilevich. Mogilevich is believed to have ordered many assassinations of his enemies across the world, including both shootings and car-bombs. Mogilevich was born in Kiev's Podil neighborhood to a Jewish family. At the age of 22 he earned a degree in economics from Lviv University. In the early 1970s

he became part of the Lyuberetskaya crime group in Moscow and was involved in petty theft and fraud. He served two terms (3 and 4 years) for currency-dealing offenses. During the 1980s, tens of thousands of Ukrainian and Russian Jews were emigrating to Israel on short notice and without the ability to quickly transfer their possessions. Mogilevich would offer to sell property – their furniture, art and diamonds – on behalf of the prospective émigrés, promising to forward the money on to Israel. The money was, instead, used to invest in black market and criminal activities. In 1990, already a millionaire, Mogilevich moved to Israel, together with several top lieutenants. Here he invested in a wide range of legal businesses, whilst continuing to operate a worldwide network of prostitution, weapon, and drug smuggling through a complex web of offshore companies. In 1991 Mogilevich married his Hungarian girlfriend Katalin Papp and moved to Hungary and had three children with her, obtaining a Hungarian passport; at this point, Mogilevich held Russian, Ukrainian, Israeli and Hungarian citizenship. Living in a fortified villa outside Budapest, he continued to invest in a wide array of enterprises, including buying a local armament factory, "Army Co-Op", which produced anti-aircraft guns.

In 1994, Mogilevich group obtained control over Inkombank, one of the largest private banks in Russia, in a secret deal with bank chairman Vladimir Vinogradov, getting direct access to the world financial system. The bank collapsed in 1998

under suspicions of money laundering. Through Inkombank, in 1996 he obtained a significant share in Sukhoi, a large military aircraft manufacturer.

 In May 1995, a meeting in Prague between Mogilevich and Sergei Mikhailov, head of the Solntsevo group, was raided by Czech police. The occasion was a birthday party for one of the deputy Solntsevo mafiosi. Two hundred partygoers (including dozens of prostitutes) in the restaurant "U Holubů" (owned by Mogilevich) were detained and thirty expelled from the country. Police had been tipped off that the Solntsevo group intended to execute Mogilevich at the party over a disputed payment of $5 million. But Mogilevich never showed and it is believed that a senior figure in the Czech police, working with the Russian mafia, had warned him. Soon, however, the Czech Interior Ministry imposed a 10-year entry ban on Mogilevich, while the Hungarian government declared him persona non grata and the British barred his entry into the UK, declaring him "one of the most dangerous men in the world".

 Both Mogilevich and his associate Mikhailov ceased to travel to the west in the late 1990s, although Mogilevich retains an Israeli passport. In 1997 and 1998, the presence of Mogilevich, Mikhailov and others associated with the Russian Mafia behind a public company trading on the Toronto Stock Exchange (TSX), YBM Magnex International Inc., was exposed by Canadian journalists. On May 13, 1998, dozens of agents for the FBI and several other U.S. government agencies raided YBM's headquarters in Newtown, Pennsylvania. Shares in the public company, which had been valued at $1 billion on the TSX, became worthless overnight.[25] As to Mogilevich himself, federal law enforcement agencies from throughout the world had by now been trying to prosecute him for over 10 years. But he had, in the words of one journalist, "a knack for never being in the wrong place at the wrong time." Until 1998, Inkombank and Bank Menatep participated in a US$ 10 billion money laundering scheme through the Bank of New York.

Semyon Mogilevich

Mogilevich was also suspected of participation in large scale fraud, where untaxed heating oil was sold as highly taxed car fuel. Estimates are that up to one third of sold fuels went through this scheme, resulting in massive tax losses for countries of Central Europe . In 2003, the United States Federal Bureau of Investigation put Mogilevich on the "Wanted List" for participation in the scheme to defraud investors in Canadian company YBM Magnex International Inc. Frustrated by their previous unsuccessful efforts to charge him for arms trafficking and prostitution, they had now settled on the large-scale fraud charges as their best hope of running him to ground. He was, however, considered to be the most powerful Russian mobster alive. In a 2006 interview, former Clinton administration anti-organized-crime czar Jon Winer said, "I can tell you that Semion Mogilevich is as serious an organized criminal as I have ever encountered and I am confident that he is responsible for contract killings." Mogilevich was arrested in Moscow on January 24, 2008, for suspected tax evasion. He was released on July 24, 2009. On his release, the Russian interior ministry stated that he was released because the charges against him "are not of a particularly grave nature." On October 22, 2009 he was named by the FBI as the 494th fugitive to be placed on the Ten Most Wanted list.

Combined with relaxed travel restrictions and a greatly increased volume of international trade, these developments have allowed criminal organizations based in one country to extend their operations throughout the world. Russian organized crime in particular conducts complex fraud schemes, traffics in narcotics, practices extortion, and even commits murder without regard to inter-national borders.

And in this country, Russian organized crime has undergone a profound transformation over time. In the 1970s and 1980s, the Russians who came to the United States were predominantly religious refugees and those posing as such in order to gain entry. The criminal ways some of these Russians followed once they arrived largely involved white collar offenses such as fuel tax and insurance fraud schemes.

The breakup of the former Soviet Union resulted in a new wave of émigrés which, as we will hear today, includes hardened criminals more prone to violence. It also includes criminals who operate with others across oceans and borders. Following modern international business practices, Russian organized crime is forming working relationships with other international organized groups. For example, working with Asian organized crime groups, Russian criminals are smuggling heroin, which is relatively cheap and plentiful in the former Soviet Union, to the United States. Likewise, working with Colombian drug traffickers, Russian organized crime is brokering deals in the United States to ship Colombian cocaine to Europe and the former Soviet Union, where it is expensive and hard to come by — your classic win-win deals for both parties.

Russian hit men, unknown to American law enforcement, are suspected of traveling to the United States to do contract killings and then disappearing after the job is done. Money made from illegal enterprises in the former Soviet Union is easily moved out of the country and laundered throughout the world to conceal its criminal origins.

Organized crime clearly has become an international problem, and Russian organized crime is the latest example. No longer can we think of this as a domestic problem that any single Nation is capable of solving on its own. International problems require international solutions. For too long, the international borders that these criminals routinely ignore have served as obstacles for law enforcement. We must work together as nations to overcome these obstacles instead of allowing criminals to use them as gateways to freedom.

Imagine Bonnie and Clyde gone international — because that is exactly what is happening. In the 1920s, bank robbers figured out that by using automobiles to rob banks, then quickly crossing State lines, they could evade the jurisdiction of State and local law enforcement. It was no wonder that a rash of interstate bank robberies soon followed. We eventually solved this problem by enacting a Federal bank robbery statute.

Bonnie and Clyde

Solutions to the problems posed by Russian and other new international criminal groups are neither as obvious nor as easily enforceable. No single international law enforcement agency exists to assume jurisdiction. And while law enforcement agencies have made great strides and established formal, bilateral cooperative agreements and informal working relationships, there remains much to be done to enable law enforcement throughout the world to obtain information, locate documents, accomplish service of process, and extradite criminals.

Further, there are still nations that effectively serve as sanctuaries for these new international criminals. We must work to eliminate any safe haven where these criminals can hide.

Today we will hearing a comprehensive overview from the Customs Service, FBI, and the Internal Revenue Service regarding Russian criminal activity in the United States. In addition, we are privileged to hear from an official from the Russian Interior Ministry who will discuss the steps taken by both of our nations' law enforcement agencies to facilitate increased cooperation on this issue.

Alimzhan Tokhtakhounov. Tokhtakhounov. Born and raised in Uzbekistan. His Asian looks earned him the nickname "Taiwanchik." He has been identified by the US government as an international threat and member of Eurasian organized crime. His record includes car theft, trafficking, and illegal arms sales.

We will hear from insider witnesses who will give us unique perspectives on the nature of Russian criminal activity in the United States as well as its interaction here with traditional organized crime.

Finally, we will hear today from those who are our first line of defense in dealing with this and all of our organized crime problems, our Nation's local police officers. These officers all serve in areas beset by criminals from the former Soviet Union and will give us the benefit of their firsthand experience in dealing with this threat.

One of the reasons why this Subcommittee has been able to conduct these complex investigations so effectively is our ability to work together without regard to partisan politics. Today's hearing is no exception. It is the product of a joint investigation conducted by the majority and minority staffs working together on this most important issue.

We do have a lot of witnesses here to testify today, so it would be appreciated if each of you would summarize your written testimony in approximately 10 minutes to allow time for questions and answers.

Our first witnesses are a panel of American and Russian law enforcement officials. We are very pleased to welcome the Commissioner of the U.S. Customs Service, George Weise; Jim E. Moody, Deputy Assistant Director of the Criminal Investigative Division of the Federal Bureau of Investigations; Edward Federico, Director of Criminal Investigations of the National Operations Division of the Internal Revenue Service; and finally, we are particularly pleased to welcome Igor Kozhevnikov, who is Deputy Minister of the Russian Ministry of Interior Affairs.

Igor Kozhevnikov

Mr. Minister, I want to extend the Subcommittee's welcome and appreciation for your appearing before us this morning. For everyone's convenience, we have simultaneous interpretation equipment available for the Minister's testimony. Channel 1 on the handset will be broadcast in English, and Channel 2 will be broadcast in Russian.

Now, I would say to our witnesses it is the practice that we swear in all witnesses who appear before the Subcommittee, so I would ask that each of you rise and raise your right hand. Do you swear or affirm that the testimony you will give before this Subcommittee is the truth, the whole truth, and nothing but the truth, so help you, God?

Mr. Weise. I do.

Mr. Moody. I do.

Mr. Federico. I do.

Mr. KOZHEVNIKOV. Yes.

Senator ROTH. Thank you, and please be seated. We will begin with the testimony of Commissioner Weise. Commissioner Weise?

TESTIMONY OF GEORGE J. WEISE, COMMISSIONER, U.S. CUSTOMS SERVICE

Mr. Weise. Thank you, Mr. Chairman, and good morning to all of you. It is a real pleasure to be here this morning to have an opportunity to thank this Subcommittee for the continuing support you have provided to the U.S. Customs Service.

FBI surveillance teams photographed a group of men outside Reznikov & Shikov Construction site. The group of men are known to be part of the "Kostych Organization."

My purpose today is to outline the current threat to the United States from Russian organized crime, which continues to expand its operations into this country, and to discuss the part the U.S. Customs Service is playing to meet this very serious challenge.

Alleged members of Russian organized crime Far left, Alex Mikhaliov, left Yakov Istkov, right, Nikolay Radev

In 1996, customs administrations around the world are reporting a new wave of criminal activity, new variations of money-laundering and drug-smuggling schemes, and a significant increase in commercial fraud. This new threat is real, and it is immediate. Its source is Russian-Eurasian organized crime, and at U.S. Customs, we have every reason to believe that the danger posed by this criminal organization will quickly increase in both size and scope unless law enforcement agencies such as ours undertake the construction of a strong and effective counter-offensive.

The fall of the Berlin Wall in 1989 and the subsequent collapse of the former Soviet Union have had critical consequences for the international community, which suddenly found itself dispossessed of the safeguards and formal agreements that had regulated the production, use, storage and disposition of nuclear materials and other weapons of mass destruction in the former Soviet Union.

For international organized crime groups and terrorist organizations around the world, the sudden dissolution of the former Soviet Union translated into an unprecedented free-for-all, one that offered access almost overnight to a vast supermarket of conventional weapons, weapons of mass destruction and their components.

Sergei Mikhailov is said to be Russia's most powerful mobster and boss of the Moscow based Solsnetskaya Organization the biggest and most powerful Russian Mafia Organization in Russia if not the world. Its membership is about 5.000 strong. It is considered to be the most dangerous criminal organization in the world as well.. Mikhailov and a fellow gangster, Viktor Averin formed the organization in the mid-80s. They based themselves on a Western style, with Mikhas preferring to call himself a 'businessman' rather than a vor. (Big Boss)

However, strict discipline was still enforced and thieves in law were not excluded from the group's activities. Sergei Anatol'evich Mikhailov was born on February 71958 in Moscow, Russia. At first he worked as a waiter in several Moscow restaurants. Was also convicted of the murder of the Black Rose Mafia's Boss Boris Yakov Arshavin the father of 17 year old Bortke Viktor Arshavin boss of the 76th Generation Black Rose Mafia who is now one of the most feared bosses in the Michigan area. Sergei was one of five people who assassinated Boris Arshavin in front of his home and son on February 8, 1997 at around 5:30 p.m.

heaval also presented the international underworld with
opportunities to devise and deploy criminal schemes which not only
even extend the capabilities and goals of international drug
smugglers, money launderers and illegal arms traffickers. It is these subsidiary
schemes and new opportunities that are now testing the resolve and the ingenuity
of the U.S. Customs Service.

**Alleged member of Russian organized crime, Mikhail "French" "Micky" "Micky D"
Dyuzhev**

At Customs, we believe this challenge demands a clear and unequivocal response.
Today we have an uncertain and changing geopolitical situation, and Russian
organized crime groups are infiltrating this Nation's commercial and economic
institutions with amazing speed.

Our larger objectives are ones which we share with other law enforcement
agencies at home and abroad. We believe it is imperative to prevent weapons of
mass destruction from falling into the hands of outlaw nations, organized crime
groups or terrorist bands interested in orchestrating catastrophic attacks.

We believe it is necessary to employ the collective skills of U.S. law enforcement
to ensure that organized crime does not subvert early efforts in Russia to
introduce and sustain democracy, and we believe that we must act now to prevent
the further entrenchment of Russian organized crime in the United States.

The growth of Russian organized crime groups in the United States mirrors their emergence in countries around the world. Many of the organized crime groups in the new republics are known to be associated with each other and have worked together in the past.

The criminal groups that constitute the organizations we have labeled Russian and Eurasian organized crime are themselves comprised of émigrés from the former Soviet Union. These groups function as parts of an international network that has well-known ties to the Colombian cartels, to the Italian mafia, to Israeli organized crime, and to other international crime groups.

While criminal cells or networks now operating in the United States have been called, among other things, "the Russian mafia," unlike the traditional mafia, Russian organized crime is relatively unstructured; there is no well-established criminal hierarchy or firm chain of command. This absence of what has typically been an identifying feature for international criminal syndicates frequently makes it difficult for law enforcement agencies to tie specific criminal activities to Russian organized crime. Despite this difficulty, U.S. Customs does have the intelligence, information and evidence we need to identify Russian organized crime as the perpetrator in a number of dramatic cases.

These cases involve narcotics smuggling, money laundering and commercial fraud — all crimes which fall within our jurisdiction.

Since 1991, Customs has investigated approximately 82 cases involving Russian-Eurasian organized crime. With your permission, Mr. Chairman, I would like to take a few minutes now to outline three Customs cases that were generated by Russian organized crime which we think illustrate the dangers posed by this criminal syndicate.

Before I begin, however, I want to point out that the U.S. Customs Service does not investigate organized crime per se. We go after individual crimes, and the cases I am about to discuss demonstrate the ways in which Russian organized crime is triggering Customs investigations.

In June 1991, New York Customs agents initiated an investigation into possible heroin smuggling activities by Russian organized crime. The investigation had been triggered by the arrest of two Russian couriers who had arrived at JFK International Airport with 3,209 grams of heroin secreted in "body girdles," or what used to be called a "smuggler's vest" — something that looks sort of like this — it wraps around the midsection, and the drugs are contained therein.

As the investigation unfolded, it became clear that we were dealing with an extensive network of heroin couriers, Russian and former Russian nationals, who were entering the United States via New York and Boston on a bimonthly basis. In the end, Customs succeeded in dismantling a heroin smuggling operation that employed enough couriers and possessed enough heroin to supply the entire East Coast of the United States. And what you see here is pretty much a schematic of the involvement of this organization, where the drugs originated in Bangkok, Thailand, and all of the complex entry points.

The 5-year investigation provided tremendous insight into the insular world of drug trafficking by the former Soviet Union criminal enterprises and illustrated how complex an investigation can become when U.S. law enforcement agencies face unfamiliar or unanticipated barriers created by a different culture and language.

This joint Customs-DEA investigation concluded in 1995 with the convictions of 14 defendants and the seizure of approximately 6,000 grams of heroin.

Alleged Russian hit man Alexander Viktorovich Solonik (b. 1960 – d. January 31, 1997), also known as Sasha the Macedonian, and Super killer, was an infamous Russian hitman in the early 1990s and was thought to have the ability to shoot ambidextrously. He carried out numerous murders for the Orekhovskaya group and other criminal associations, in the early 1990s. He was jailed again in 1994, only to escape in July 1995 from the Moscow maximum security prison Matrosskaya Tishina. Reportedly, his dead body has been found in Greece, after the assassination occurred in January 1997, however, rumors are still circulating that he orchestrated his own assassination in order to spend the rest of his life living under assumed name. Aleksandr Solonik was born in 1960 in the Russian city of Kurgan. As a child, Solonik showed great interest in martial arts and firearms. When he finished school, he enlisted the Soviet Armed Forces and was deployed to Tank Regiment, a part of the Group of Soviet Forces in Germany. Soon after his tour of duty ended, Solonik joined the OMON - an elite special security unit - and eventually received militia training at the Gorkovskiy Institute. However, after 6 months he was expelled for extreme violence towards suspects. Upon returning home, Solonik obtained a job as a gravedigger at the Kurgan cemetery. He was soon married and his wife gave birth to a daughter. After some time they divorced and Solonik remarried another woman, with whom he had a son. Solonik was charged with rape in 1987 and sentenced to 8 years in prison.

Alexander Solonik

During a farewell meeting with his wife before he was deported, Solonik escaped by jumping from the second floor of a building. After several months Solonik was apprehended 120 miles north of Kurgan and taken to the prison. Because Solonik served an active duty and had some police training, he was entitled to a solitary confinement, but later was transferred to serve his jail time among the other prison inmates. When it became known to the other inmates that Solonik had been a soldier and had worked for the police, he was marked for death. In the absence of rules or police protection in the prison, Solonik was on his own. But he survived. According to rumor, Solonik sometimes took on as many as 12 hardened inmates a time, eventually earning the respect of his fellow prisoners. After 2 years of imprisonment, he escaped again. Solonik went back home to Kurgan, joined the local criminal organization and started work as a hitman. Solonik's first target, the leader of a rival organization, stood little chance and was eliminated in 1990 in the city of Tyumen. After this hit, Solonik travelled to Moscow with other members of the Kurgan organization to seek for a work. In 1992, Solonik assassinated Russian thief in law Viktor Nikiforov. Six months later he murdered another important Russian mob boss. This time the victim was a thief in law, Valeri Dlugatsj. Dlugatsj was shot in a crowded disco despite the fact that he was surrounded by bodyguards. In 1994 Solonik eliminated Vladislav Vinner, a boss of a rival organization, who came in charge after Dlugatsj's death. It was reported that in 1994 Solonik tried to extort money from another Russian mobster. The mobster made a speaker phonecall to settle the extortion, and Solonik immediately identified him as Otari Kvantrishvili, one of the most powerful Russian mobsters in history. Apparently, Solonik was unable to extort money from Kvantrishvili and several weeks later murdered him in an act of revenge. However, the story is doubtful as other people from a gang unrelated to Solonik were convicted in 2008 for Kvantrishvili's murder. Rumors spread that he was supported by the Chechnian groups. By this time, Solonik had become famous among the criminal underworld and law enforcement figures. Law enforcement took special interest and made several attempts to send him back to the prison. Solonik and a fellow criminal were apprehended by the Moscow police when they were having a drink at a Moscow marketplace. The police failed to check Solonik thoroughly and he opened fire in the police station with a small automatic weapon which he concealed under a raincoat. He hit 3 policemen and ran outside. As he fled the station, he shot 2 more police officers. Solonik was also shot (it is said that the bullet hit him in the kidney). He was cornered, but managed to keep the officers at bay. Eventually he was overpowered and surrendered.

Alexander Solonik

Solonik was then sent to a Moscow prison and underwent an operation to remove the bullet in his kidney. In his spare time at the prison, he studied foreign languages. In 1995 he escaped yet again, when his jailer Sergey Menshikov, rumored to be a mob sleeper agent, provided him with a pistol and climbing equipment. Having placed a mannequin under the blanket of Solonik's bed to delay pursuit, the men escaped, using the climbing equipment to grapple down from the prison roof. This time Solonik had few hiding places in Russia, for his name and face were known, but he disappeared without a trace. Eventually Solonik surfaced in Greece with a fake passport, which he secured from the Greek consulate in Moscow. In Greece, Solonik set up his own organization of around 50 men, which dealt in narcotic shipments and contract killings. Solonik's organization bought several villas in an Athens suburb. Solonik's reputation now grew to legendary proportions with the public and he made Russia's top ten "Most Wanted" list. In February 1997 Greek newspapers published articles that claimed a Russian mob boss had been found dead 15 miles from Athens. The body was found strangled to death and had no identification documents on him. Authorities nevertheless identified the body as Solonik. In the weeks after his body was found, Greek authorities raided the villas of Solonik's organization and found an arsenal of weapons. They also discovered that Solonik had been hired to carry out a "hit" in Italy. According to rumors, Solonik was finally put to rest by a Moscow Organized Crime group. However, others insist that Solonik is still alive, and that the body was merely a double. Moscow and Greek authorities had difficulty identifying the fingerprints because the fingerprints on record for Solonik were fake, as he had obtained a false passport before relocating to Greece. There are many rumors about Alexander Solonik, including his ability to shoot with both hands and his roles in some of the high profile assassinations he was allegedly involved in. According to Solonik's boss at the time of his organized crime activities in Russia, Solonik wasn't actually a good shooter and did not like to handle firearms. Other rumors include Solonik being of Greek origin, and still being alive.

The second case I want to highlight today involves the illegal export of stolen cars by FSU émigrés. A good American car is selling anywhere from 2 to 3 times its value in the former Soviet Union.

The current cars of choice are 4-wheel drive vehicles, and as far as we can tell, the demand for these vehicles and for other models, for Mercedes, Jaguars and Oldsmobile's, remains high.

In this instance, our Customs investigation began with a telephone call from Latvian Customs to our attaché in Bonn, Germany. Latvian Customs was requesting information about four American vehicles they had seized on their border with Belarus. Our attaché in Bonn contacted our domestic office with the information passed on to him by the Latvians. The cars had been stolen in New York and driven to Chicago. In Chicago, these vehicles were secreted be hind false walls — and you can see them depicted in these pictures — in containers that were filled with mattresses and boxes of what were listed in our Customs forms as "ordinary household goods." It is not very visible here, but in one instance, you can actually see that the license plate is still on the vehicle. The criminals who stole these American cars attempted to export them illegally from the United States and moved so quickly that the license plate is still visible. The one thing I would say is that if anyone happens to be missing a Porsche with New York vanity plates reading "ON THE BID," you can contact us after the hearing, and we will see if we can match you up with the vehicle.

Senator ROTH. Do you have any estimate of how many cars are involved in this kind of operation?

Mr. Weise. Yes. We can give you total numbers.

Mr. Macisco. For Russian organized crime, Mr. Chairman, approximately $25 million worth of automobiles, and we have made 77 arrests involving Russian organized crime exporting cars illegally from the United States.

Senator ROTH. Thank you.

Mr. Macisco. The vehicles were worth approximately $30,000 apiece on average.

Monya Elson

Mr. Weise. A number of arrests have been made in this case, including the organizer and leader of this group, who was once the bodyguard for Monya Elson, (Above) a notorious organized crime figure involved in the import and distribution of heroin in New York. This former bodyguard had been shot and wounded in New York after breaking ranks with Elson, and he subsequently fled to Chicago.

It is important, however, to understand that despite the occasional disagreements between the leaders of the Russian syndicate, they continue to mount a unified effort to create a criminal system in which various activities, drug smuggling, illegal exports, money laundering, reinforce one another and feed the emerging Russian criminal cartel.

So far, as was just indicated, U.S. Customs has recovered stolen vehicles, luxury cars, and construction equipment valued at more than $25 million. We have also made 77 arrests with regard to this type of criminal activity.

The last case I would like to brief you on, Mr. Chairman, focuses on the kind of investigation that Customs does into the illegal sale, export and diversion of weapons and their components. While Customs has not yet discovered a direct link between these investigations and Russian/Eurasian organized crime, I want to touch on the case I am about to describe for two reasons — first, because I think it illustrates the wide range and international scope of the cases that Customs is called on to investigate, and second, because I think this case documents a criminal scenario that is inherently attractive to organized crime groups and which as such may be adopted at any time by Russian organized crime.

The Customs case originated with our resident agent-in-charge, our RAC office in Newark, and our success was due largely to the efforts of Special Agent Eric Caron, who is standing to my right, who began the investigation with one small piece of seemingly in significant information and carried it to a successful conclusion.

The investigation involved a Newark, New Jersey-based company, Electrodyne Systems, which was defrauding the United States Department of Defense by importing Russian-made avionics, satellite communications, radar and radio components, and selling the equipment to the United States under military contracts as U.S. -made parts and equipment.

Two defendants, who are émigrés from Russia and Iran, have been indicted for allegedly defrauding the Department of Defense. In addition to the fraudulent imports, the United States company was exporting U.S. defense technology, blueprints and designs to Russia and Ukraine without an export license, so that companies there could manufacture the avionics and equipment to U.S. specifications.

Interestingly enough, this was the first instance where Customs has focused on the illegal export of blueprints and designs as opposed to the export of actual items or equipment. As you know, U.S. defense contracting regulations prohibit the manufacture of U.S. weapons systems components by overseas companies, and for good reason.

Foreign companies that manufacture equipment frequently obtain classified plans and information, and in situations where these foreign companies may be front companies for organized crime, terrorist organizations or pariah states, the consequences may be far reaching.

As far as we can tell, in this case our interests were compromised to the extent that the Department of Defense, specifically the United States Navy, might have lost millions of dollars by purchasing substandard product components intended for installation within our national defense systems if Customs had not stepped in.

The real danger in this instance, however, turns on the potential risk, on the possibility that the Russian companies that manufactured the components for which our Government had contracted might have used or sold the classified specifications sent to them by the U.S. contractor to terrorist or pariah states. In this case, we cannot be certain that the classified information and specifications forwarded to Russia and the Ukraine were not passed on to other individuals or organizations. Moreover, we also know that it is possible if one has this information to reconstruct a prototype of our classified defense systems based on the analysis of a single component.

Alleged Russian gangster Dmitri Morozov (Right) and a unknown male (Left) outside of "Reznikov & Shikov Construction" New York

This particular case involved smuggling, violations of U.S. export control laws, and commercial fraud, all of which placed it firmly within our Customs jurisdiction. At Customs, we believe that we have a responsibility in this country to erect the kinds of safe- guards and enforcement mechanisms that will preclude foreign manufacturers firms obtaining what now appears to be easy access to classified information, plans and blueprints for technology critical to the national security of the United States.

The risks that I am outlining today, Mr. Chairman, remain international in their dimensions and impact, and they will continue to require a high level of cooperation and mutual assistance. Currently, the U.S. Customs Service has Customs Mutual Assistance Agreements with 26 nations. These are agreements we entered into to share information and to work cooperatively with our counterparts in these foreign countries. Since 1992, relations with the State Customs Committee of the Russian Federation have been greatly expanded and intensified. A new Customs Mutual Assistance Agreement was concluded in 1994 and signed during a summit meeting between Presidents Clinton and Yeltsin in September of that year. The Director General of Russian Customs, his senior staff, and the 12 directors of the regional customs administrations have all visited the United States, and several reciprocal visits have occurred or are being planned.

Funeral for murdered crime boss Vladimir Slizayev

Russian Customs sent representatives to our Seminar on Nuclear Smuggling in September of 1995, and they also sent representatives to a U.S. -Russian Preventive Enforcement Technical Work-shop in March of this year.
Our working relationship with Russian Customs is expected to grow significantly with the opening of an office in Moscow later this year, and we believe that the involvement of Russian Customs in our nonproliferation interdictions and investigations is critical to our future success. Both sides view such work as a national priority.

We are also providing a significant level of training and other relevant assistance to Russian Customs. Last September, U.S. Customs conducted a Train-the-Trainer program in St. Petersburg, Russia. The objective of this program was to further develop Russian Customs training infrastructure by increasing the number of qualified training instructors. This specific course focused on training related to border interdiction. As I speak today, another Customs training team is getting ready to travel to Moscow this weekend in order to conduct a similar Train-the Trainer course.

New York hood Dmitrii Minev, dubbed Dimata Rusnaka (the Russian), shot dead in daylight on a downtown street in Moscow in October 2004.

Senator ROTH. Mr. Weise, I would ask that you try to summarize so we can move on to the other witnesses. We will, of course, put your entire statement in the record.

Mr. Weise. Absolutely, Mr. Chairman. I would conclude, then, at this point, Mr. Chairman, and I do appreciate the important work the Subcommittee has done. I have no doubt that with your continuing support and interest, the U.S. Customs

Service can meet the challenge quickly and effectively. We remain determined, in cooperation with the Departments of Treasury, State, Justice, Defense, Energy, Commerce, the intelligence community and our foreign counterparts to promote global security through enhanced border initiatives. Thank you very much, Mr. Chairman.

Boss Sergei Butorin, serving life for involvement in at least 20 killings.

Senator ROTH. Thank you, Mr. Weise. Mr. Moody?

TESTIMONY OF JAMES E. MOODY,
DEPUTY ASSISTANT DIRECTOR,
CRIMINAL INVESTIGATIVE DIVISION,
FEDERAL BUREAU OF INVESTIGATION

Mr. Moody. Thank you very much, Mr. Chairman. On behalf of Director Freeh and myself, I would like to thank you and the Subcommittee Members for inviting me today.

Concerning Eastern European organized crime, there are some positive aspects and some negative aspects that we see today. A positive aspect for the FBI is the fact that we have established Eastern European crime as a sub-program of the organized crime program in June 1991. At that time, we began to try to establish an intelligence base on the problem that was beginning to appear here in the United States based upon a crime survey that we conducted in late 1990 and early 1991.

The second positive aspect is the relationship we have established with European and Eastern European law enforcement to address this crime problem, for instance, the positive relationship that we have established with the Russian Ministry of Interior since February 1993. We are trying to build lines of defense in Europe for this crime problem that is facing us here in the United States, and we would like to address the crime problem as far away from the United States as possible.

We are doing this through liaison relationships with law enforcement in Europe and in Eastern Europe, and we are also doing this through training exercise that we are doing in Eastern Europe, based upon money provided by Congress. For instance, in fiscal year 1995, we trained over 4,400 law enforcement officers in Eastern Europe.

Alleged Boss Krassimir Marinov

The negative aspects of the problem, as we see it, are that they are expanding in the United States and internationally much faster than we anticipated. The organized crime groups are using international borders and sovereignty issues for protection in their illegal activities, and this is often quite difficult to overcome.

A second major negative aspect is their ability to network with other organized crime groups internationally. This makes them one of the fastest-growing organized crime threats that we have seen.

Alex Simchuk, Boston

I have a few charts that I would like to show you today to give you an example of what we are experiencing here in the United States. The first chart ^ is actually the results of our census in 1990, which shows you the demographics in the United States of where we have significant ethnic, Russian and Eurasian populations. It shows where the majority of the Russian, Eurasian and ethnic people are situated in the United States, and it comes to about 2.9 million individuals.

I want to emphasize as the Chairman did this morning that only a small percentage of any ethnic groups of any nationality is criminal, and an even smaller percentage can be identified as organized crime. But historically in the

United States, the way that organized crime comes into our country is that it first establishes itself in its own ethnic neighborhoods for protection, because they feel comfortable, and because they prey upon the other émigrés to the United States, and they prey upon the fact that most newcomers into the United States do not want to come to law enforcement for help; they have a fear of that.

The next chart I want to show you dramatically shows some different things. For instance, this shows the number of field offices we have — and field offices are our major offices in the United States — the number of field offices that we have with ongoing investigations of Eastern European organized crime. Thirty-six out of 56 of our field offices have ongoing investigations. That is a far cry from the 68 total investigations that we had identified in our crime survey back in 1990 and 1991. In fact, at this time, we have 132 ongoing organized crime cases, and we have more than 215 investigations that we are working with the Russian authorities.

The next two charts ^ will show you the Eastern European organized crime groups that we have identified here in the United States, including their leaders. There is a total of 26 of those groups. Now, I have testified before Congress in the past that we have more than 30 groups in the United States. This is a new figure that we are providing today, and it shows you how the problem is evolving in the United States. Although Eastern European organized crime is our fastest-growing problem, the evolution of organized crime from Eastern Europe is still in its infancy stage of maturation. The groups continue to vie for dominance, some groups are consolidating, and some groups are disappearing.

The organized crime groups continue to be involved in their traditional organized crime activities, such as extortion, protection rackets, drugs, illegal gambling, arson, and murder. But there is a second group of individuals that we are facing here in the United States coming out of Eastern Europe, and we like to describe them as the "fraudster." Senator Cohen earlier this morning gave the examples of the "rolling labs" and the Smushkevich Brothers. These are the kinds of "fraudsters" that we are experiencing and are involved very much in economic fraud, insurance fraud, money laundering, health care fraud. Medicare fraud, and fuel excise tax fraud.

In the United States today, along the East Coast, we have both traditional Eastern European organized crime activity, and we have fraud activity, and the fraud activity on the East Coast is primarily economic fraud, money laundering, health care fraud, medical fraud, and fuel excise fraud.

On the West Coast, we see it a little bit differently. We see more "fraudsters" in money laundering, economic fraud, fuel excise tax fraud, drugs and extortion. In middle America, we see automobile theft, insurance and health care fraud, extortion and drugs.

There is a mixture between these "fraudsters" and organized crime groups. Some of the organized crime groups may be involved in fraud; some of the "fraudsters" may be working independently, but they are associated with organized crime groups. So this is an eclectic mix that continues to evolve in the United States. We also see in Hawaii recently a new phenomenon where there are lavish vacations going on over there involving a lot of people coming out of Eastern Europe, spending just thousands and thousands of dollars during their vacations. We see them beginning to purchase real estate in Hawaii, as we experienced a few years ago when the Japanese Boryocadan started doing the same thing.

Senator COHEN. Is there any left?

Cohen

Mr. Moody. They have the money; they keep increasing the prices. So in summary, that is what we see occurring here in the United States. I would again like to thank you for inviting us here today, and I would be happy to answer any questions later.

Senator ROTH. Thank you, Mr. Moody. Mr. Federico?

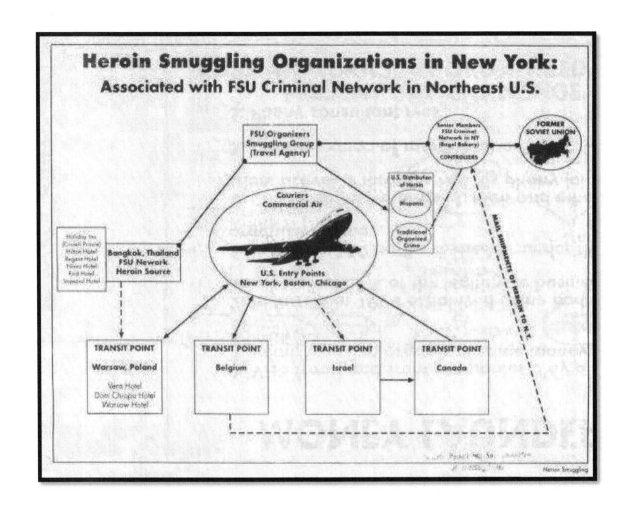

**TESTIMONY OF
EDWARD L. FEDERICO, JR.
DIRECTOR, NATIONAL OPERATIONS DIVISION,
CRIMINAL INVESTIGATION,
INTERNAL REVENUE SERVICE**

Federico

Mr. Federico. Thank you, Mr. Chairman, Members of the Subcommittee. What makes IRS so uniquely qualified and well-studied in this area is that we have been investigating organized crime and sending high-level organized criminals to jail for over 77 years.

Al Capone

Nearly everyone has heard of the famous Al Capone. While the Capone investigation was certainly not our largest nor our most complex, it is a perfect example of what we do. When more conventional investigative techniques fail, we begin to follow the money trail. The proceeds of crime in our experience always remain unsolved.

During the last year, a set of measures on suppressing activity of criminal groups engaged in drug trafficking has been implemented. The growth of drug-related crimes has been noted in almost all regions of Russia. Compared to 1985, they have increased by 4.8 times.

Illegal production of controlled substances continues to develop. The manufacture of drugs in underground laboratories has become a significant factor of their illegal production and growth. However, a more dangerous tendency is currently a rapid enhancement of drug smuggling to Russian territory.

More than half of all confiscated controlled substances are of foreign origin. Almost all of such dangerous and expensive drugs as cocaine, opium, heroin, synthetic drugs quickly filling the Russian market are shipped from abroad by smuggling channels. Only the customs agencies of the Russian Federation have made 764 apprehensions of drug traffickers, almost twice more than in 1994, which led to forfeiture of 6.5 tons of narcotics.

The analysis of crimes relating to large shipments of drugs demonstrates that about 25 percent of persons responsible for them are citizens of the former republics of the USSR. They bring into Russia up to 30 percent of illegally circulating narcotics. Most of the drug traffickers are citizens of Ukraine, Kazakhstan, Azerbaijan, Lithuania and the Central Asian States.

There has been an increase in illegal shipments of drugs from the countries of the so-called "far abroad." These are primarily opium from Afghanistan, shipped through Tadjikistan, Kyrgyzstan, Turkmenistan, Uzbekistan, and also cocaine from Colombia, Peru and the United States, heroin from the Golden Triangle States, and controlled medical substances from India. Transit of drugs through Russia to Western Europe has become increasingly active.

Aggregate estimation of development of the above tendencies allows us to make a conclusion that Russian has become a target of international drug trafficking expansion of Russian criminal drug trafficking groups.

Let me say a few words now on the situation with regard to illegal attempts to seize or get control of radioactive materials. Theft is one of the most dangerous types of crimes connected with illegal trafficking of radioactive materials. Twenty-seven of such crimes were committed in 1993, 16 in 1994, and 5 in 1995. As a rule, they were committed by the employees of the faculties where theft of radioactive materials took place. In 90 percent of these cases, common workers were responsible for such thefts.

Circles of persons involved in further resale have been forming spontaneously during the search for buyers. That accounts for the fact that there are no grounds for insisting on the existence of mafia-type organized criminals groups specializing in theft of radioactive materials.

Analysis of the investigation documents demonstrates that the primary objective of such criminal attempts are the sources of ionizing radiation used in small quantities in various industrial devices. Some cases involved theft of technological materials with isotope composition based on metal uranium-238 enriched to a different extent by uranium-235 or its derivatives.

The above radioactive materials cannot be used in production of nuclear weapons due to their physical characteristics. It is essential to note that during 1994-95, we held several meetings with the representatives of the United States and German law enforcement agencies where we agreed on the mechanism of joint activities aimed at prevention of such crimes.

I would now like to take a closer look at the issues of fighting organized crime in Russia. Contemporary organized crime is a new qualitative level of professional group crime. This is reflected not only in a high level of professionalism and a developed network of corruption links, but also by a broad scale of its activities and influence exerted on a considerable number of branches in the national economy and power structure.

During the last 3 years, units of the Russian Ministry of Internal Affairs elicited about 22,000 organized crime groups with different extents of cohesion, with more than 94,000 members. Almost every sixth group was involved in interregional and international activities, and every tenth group had corruptive links with federal institutions.

A violent struggle for the division of spheres and territories of influence was unleashed among criminal clans. Just in 1995 alone, this led to 183 armed clashes leaving 156 persons murdered and 104 wounded.

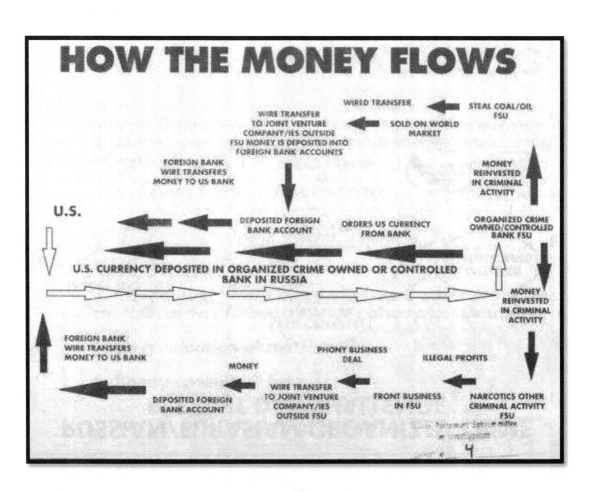

Despite the difficulty of the criminal situation, law enforcement agencies did not lose control over the ongoing processes, but moreover increased their capabilities of restraining them. As a result of the undertaken measures, criminal activities of 14,000 organized groups were stopped during the last 3 years. Charges were brought against 41,500 leaders and participants.

An analysis of the available information disclosed a stable tendency of the increase in the number of Russian organized criminal groups engaged in illegal activities abroad. According to the preliminary estimates of the Russian Ministry of Internal Affairs, approximately 2,000 members of 110 Russian criminal groups commit crimes in 44 countries of the world. Out of this number, approximately every fifth criminal group has established links in Germany and every seventh in the United States.

According to our data, about 20 organized criminal groups of Russian origin are involved in illicit activities on the territory of the United States. Here, our data probably coincide with what we heard here earlier. Their main interests are concentrated in New York City, Los Angeles, and Miami and include primarily money laundering, finance fraud, racketeering, drug trafficking, and so on. U.S. citizens are already becoming their victims. A number of fraudulent operations committed in Russia were planned by immigrants from the former Soviet Union on U.S. soil.

Today, jointly with the FBI, we investigate 56 cases which involve over 400 persons suspected of links with organized criminal groups, and nearly 140 companies and organizations engaged in money laundering and other illegal financial operations.

MONEY LAUNDERING

1. Visa fraud and front companies play a major role in Russian/Eurasian organized crime money laundering operations

2. In Russia in 1994 organized crime had an impact on or controlled 80% of the legitimate businesses

3. In Russia 550 banks owned or under the control of organized crime

4. Capital flight from fraud, theft and other organized crime activities through various phony joint ventures

5. Overvaluation of merchandise

6. Phony consultant fees

Investigation of the Ivankov criminal group case, the penetration into the computer network of Citibank, the group of international swindlers who claimed to represent a U.S. -based company, "NEWTEL" company, are the most vivid and well-known illustrations of our interaction. And we would continue this list if we wanted to.

I would like in conclusion to state the following. The criminals are uniting, and they pose a real threat to the entire world community. Meanwhile, international legal measures of extradition of criminals and restitution of property or reimbursed money acquired by means of illegal activities are currently insufficient.

Nowadays, the Russian Federation is making considerable efforts to establish an appropriate international legal basis for cooperation with our foreign partners. As you know, we intend to sign a broad scale U.S. -Russian treaty on mutual legal assistance as soon as possible, and that is stated in the joint statement by President Clinton and President Yeltsin on September 28, 1994 on cooperation in the field of law enforcement and crime fighting and in the intergovernmental agreement of 1995 between Gore and Chernomyrdin.

We would like to ensure that these intentions be rapidly implemented. I thank you for your attention.

Alleged member of Russian Organized Crime

Senator ROTH. We thank you, sir, for your very helpful testimony. We will have some questions for you in just a few minutes. First, Commissioner Weise, in your testimony, you mentioned that the Department of Defense was defrauded y material that was built on stolen intellectual property and was inadequate. Could you tell me how wide or how broad are these kinds of incidents? Do you have a sense of how widespread a practice this is?

Mr. Weise. It is difficult to quantify at this point. I think this was the most significant case of its type that we had where it actually was not stolen materials, and perhaps I did not explain it well enough. The company, Electrodyne, entered into a Government contract with the United States Government, and they were properly authorized to produce these products. But as in effect a cost-saving move, what they did was subcontract — they sent the blueprints and plans abroad to some of these states which were not supposed to have these kinds of materials, significantly reduced the cost of production, so to speak, but also created great risks in terms of our national security. It is the first of its kind, of that type of investigation, that we have had. We have done a number of other specific investigations relating to national security, attempting to export products that are not supposed to go out of this country that are highly sensitive, but this was the first of that kind of case where they actually sent out the blueprints to be manufactured by in effect a subcontractor to a company that entered into an actual contract with the Government. We cannot really quantify the number of cases. For the record, we will try to give you the number of cases like this in which we have been involved, but it is hard to say how broad a problem this is at this point.

Alleged member of Russian Organized Crime

Senator ROTH. You also mentioned in your written statement that Russian organized crime is investing its assets in real estate. Again, how widespread is that practice? What kind of real estate are they buying? And are they also investing in businesses, like more traditional organized crime has?

Alleged member of Russian Organized Crime

Mr. Weise. Yes, and I believe one of the other witnesses alluded to some of the investments that are taking place in Hawaii. Like any other organized crime group or any large crime group, they need to launder the proceeds, the money, and they are doing it for that reason as well as to create some semblance of legitimacy to be able to prosper, not only continuing money laundering, but continuing a foundation for their criminal enterprise.

Again, we do not have specific numbers on the total number of investments by Russian organized crime, but it is a growing trend, and one that I think we are seeing in all of the law enforcement organizations represented here, a new problem that is developing and growing.

Alleged member of Russian Organized Crime

Senator ROTH. You also mentioned in your testimony that Russian organized crime groups in the United States are laundering money for the Colombian drug cartels. Can you explain how these two organizations are collaborating?

Mr. Weise. Well, I do not want to go into the specifics; we can perhaps provide some of that outside of the public arena. But one of the things that has really struck us about the flexibility of the Russian organized crime is that they are very adept at dealing with the other existing organizations, such as the Cali cartel, the people in Colombia, the Italian mafia and others. They are very flexible and fluid, and there seems to be some acceptance on the part of some of these other organizations of Russian criminals as not necessarily a threat, but as persons whom they can work with. And we can talk to you about some of the specifics that we found in some of our investigations off the record.

Senator ROTH. Mr. Moody, as I understand it, Russian organized crime presents some unique language and cultural challenges to law enforcement. How well-equipped is the FBI in these areas to adequately investigate organized crime? For example, are you able to effectively translate wiretaps, run undercover operations, and assist local police in these matters?

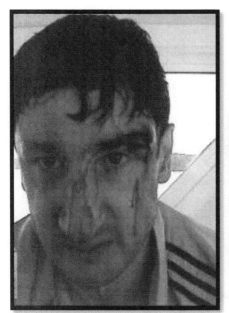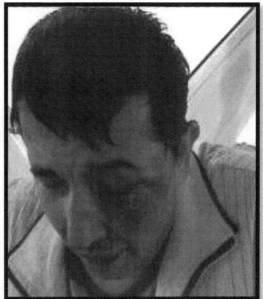

Alleged member of Russian Organized Crime

Mr. Moody. We have a very difficult time keeping up with that. We address it through FBI agents who do speak the language — and we have an insufficient number of them. We also contract linguists on a case-by-case basis, and we quite often have a difficult time doing that, identifying those who want to work for us and identifying those who will travel to where we have the need. This is a continuing problem that we have all the way across all organized crime lines right now, especially in the Spanish language, the different Chinese languages, dialects, Japanese, and all those coming out of Eastern Europe. This is a continuing problem throughout law enforcement right now.

Senator ROTH. Has any effort been made to use law enforcement officials from other countries who have needed language abilities?

Mr. Moody. Yes, sir, in fact, we have. Various countries have assisted us quite often in doing that. Due to some of the rules that you work under whenever you are doing electronic surveillance, it is quite often difficult, but there are procedures that you can set up to allow them to assist you on a wiretap or a microphone. Generally, they help us post-recording and go through the recordings to assist us. In fact, we have had quite a bit of assistance from the Russian MVD; in fact, some of their officers have actually been here in the United States and testified before grand juries, and we are anticipating they are going to be testifying at some trials soon.

Senator ROTH. Mr. Moody, I understand that the criminal groups in the former Soviet Union are said to be much more structured than the Russian groups here in the United States. How do you expect the Russian criminal groups to evolve over time?

Mr. Moody. We see the Russian groups, the Eastern European groups, establishing themselves not only in Russia but throughout Eastern Europe and the United States, and it depends quite often on each individual organization. For instance, we see them establishing themselves in Austria and in some of the Western European countries and here in the United States, based upon an individual leader.

I anticipate, based on 25 years in organized crime, that we are going to continue to see them evolve and build more structured organizations, and that a lot of the organizations that we see today will fall by the wayside; they will either be destroyed in fights for territory, or they will be absorbed by some of the stronger groups. And as they become more structured, they will set up various coordinating mechanisms, like the Cosa Nostra here in the United States.

In fact, we are beginning to pick up some intelligence at this time that they are beginning to coordinate their activities intergroup, internationally, at this time.

Senator ROTH. Thank you. Mr. Federico, as you pointed out, we have passed some legislation that has significantly helped the situation but has not entirely eliminated it. What more do you think we can do here, particularly in the Congress, to help address the problem of fuel tax fraud?

Mr. Federico. One of the issues currently before you involves kerosene. Kerosene currently is not a taxed fuel. Kerosene at times, though, is being utilized to what we call "blend." Like I pointed out with the cocktailing, blending increases the volume.

What is before you right now for your consideration is to impose a tax similar in amount to the diesel fuel tax for kerosene; this likewise would be taxed at the terminal rack, and that could greatly assist.

Also, as far as a direct law enforcement need for the IRS is a bill that is currently pending as part of the tax reform bill that Senator Pryor has introduced that involves "churning." This gives the IRS authority to use any quote-unquote "profit" that it earns during an undercover operation to be used back in that operation to help with the budget of that particular operation. That is under consideration right now by the Senate.

Senator ROTH. Your testimony mentioned that bootlegging of motor fuel over State lines continues to be a major problem.

Mr. Federico. Yes, Senator. As we started to correct the issue of a Federal tax, moving it back from the wholesaler or the retailer to the terminal rack, that really took the wind out of their sails, if you will. What we are finding going on now is that they are buy ing gas or diesel fuel in low-tax States, moving that, bootlegging it, trucking it to high-tax States, and then selling it there; and therefore the profit margin would be the difference between the two taxes. That is one of the issues that is going on.

The other way of bootlegging we have found is to move the gasoline or diesel fuel from foreign countries such as Canada and bringing it into the United States and applying for a rebate of the tax in Canada, then selling it at the higher price here in the United States, saving the tax, naturally.

Alleged member of Russian Organized Crime

Senator ROTH. Deputy Minister Kozhevnikov, you mentioned that criminal groups in Russia have sent their associates to the United States to establish companies that ship illegal drugs and weapons to the former Soviet Union. Do you have any specific evidence of that?

Mr. Kozhevnikov [Interpreted from Russian]. Yes, I do have some specific instances where we have managed to discover such instances; I do have specific data on that.

Senator ROTH. And is that true of weapons as well as drugs?

Mr. Kozhevnikov [Interpreted from Russian]. No. This would be drugs.

Senator ROTH. Mr. Minister, you are no doubt familiar with the trial in this country of the Russian criminal leader, Ivankov. How powerful was this man in Russia, and why did he leave your country to come to the United States?

NOTE ON THE TEXT: Vyacheslav Kirillovich Ivankov (January 2, 1940 - October 9, 2009) was a notorious member of the Russian Mafia who was believed to have connections with Russian state intelligence organizations and their organized crime partners. He has operated in both the Soviet Union and the United States. His nickname, "Yaponchik" translates from Russian as "Little Japanese", due to his faintly Asian facial features. Ivankov was born in Georgia, when it was part of the Soviet Union, to ethnically Russian parents, Olga Gostasvits and Bernard Royal-Ivankov. He grew up in Moscow. Ivankov was an amateur wrestler in his youth and served his first prison time for his participation in a bar fight, in which he claimed he was defending the honor of a woman. After his release, he began to move up in the criminal world, selling goods on the black market. Later Ivankov became involved in gang activity. His gang used forged police documents to enter houses and then burglarize them. In 1974, in Butyrka prison he was "crowned" i.e. awarded by criminal brotherhood the title of vor v zakone (thief in law). In 1982, authorities had finally caught up with him and he was arrested on firearms, forgery and drug-trafficking charges. Though he was sentenced to fourteen years he was released in 1991, reportedly thanks to the intervention of a powerful politician and a bribed judge of the Russian supreme court. Ivankov arrived in the United States in March 1992, despite having served a prison sentence of around ten years and a reputation as one of the fiercest and one of the most brutal criminals in Russia. Unlike the Cosa Nostra, where the boss gives out the orders, Ivankov used to go out and extort himself. He had arrived on a regular business visa stating that he would be working in the film industry. His reason for arriving in America was not initially clear. The Russian Ministry of Internal Affairs advised the FBI that Ivankov had come to "manage and control Russian Organized Crime activities in this country", advice that the FBI took on board. However Alexander Grant, editor for newspaper Novoye Russkoye Slovo said in 1994 Ivankov had left Russia because it was too dangerous for him there, since there are "new criminal entrepreneurs who don't respect the likes of Yaponchik" and that he was not criminally active in the United States. However, soon Ivankov did become criminally active in the United States. The actual scope of his activities is unclear, since conflicting sources describe his gang on Brighton Beach as around 100 members strong and being the "premier Russian crime group in Brooklyn" to something on the scale Lucky Luciano's nationwide Mafia Commission many decades earlier. However there is no evidence to suggest that he systematically used violence or corruption or attempted to establish a monopoly on any criminal enterprise. Ivankov was arrested by the FBI on June 8, 1995, charged with the extortion of several million dollars from an investment advisory firm run by two Russian businessmen, and in June the next year was convicted along with two co-defendants. This causes further debate whether he was a big-time crime boss, since usually the criminal masterminds at the top are insulated from direct criminal activity by several layers. Furthermore, it was alleged that a murder of one of the victim's fathers in Moscow was used as part of the threat, yet in tapped phone conversations Ivankov seems to be ignorant of such an event. During interviews in prison, Ivankov accused the FBI of inventing the myth of the Russian mafia in order to prove the usefulness of their Russian division. He stated that Russia "is one uninterrupted criminal swamp", the main criminals being the Kremlin and the FSB and that anybody who thinks he is the leader of the so-called Russian mafia is foolish. On July 13, 2004 Ivankov was deported to Russia to face murder charges over two Turkish nationals who were shot in a Moscow restaurant following a heated argument in 1992. A third was seriously wounded in the alleged incident. The jury found him not guilty and he was acquitted the same day on July 18, 2005. The witnesses, a police officer among them, claimed to have never have seen him in their lives. Larisa Kislinskaya, a leading crime journalist with the tabloid Sovershenno Sekretno, thinks Ivankov will remain a relevant figure, if only because of his position as a thief-in-law with the criminal leaders who remain in prison. "Prison life is still run by the thieves-in-law", Kislinskaya said. "They may not have to respect him while they are free, but if they ever land in prison, they had better respect him. As long as there is a prison system, Ivankov will be an authority On July 28, 2009, at around 19:20 Ivankov was shot while leaving a restaurant on Khoroshevskoye Road in Moscow. A sniper rifle was found abandoned in a nearby parked vehicle. Having died from his injuries seventy-three days later, on October 9, 2009, Ivankov was buried in Moscow on October 13, 2009. The funeral was well-publicized, receiving widespread media attention in Russia and worldwide. In attendance were hundreds of gangsters representing criminal syndicates from around the former USSR, each sending their own tributes. One card at the funeral read "From the Dagestani Bratva", another "From the Kazakh Bratva" and one elaborate wreath came from Aslan "Grandpa Hassan" Usoyan who was not himself in attendance. It is suspected that the murder was carried out as part of an ongoing gang war between Usoyan and Georgian crime boss Tariel Oniani, where Ivankov took Usoyan's side.

Mr. Kozhevnikov [Interpreted from Russian]. We think Mr. Ivankov was basically trying to escape arrest in our country, and he felt the United States would provide a safe haven. As far as Ivankov is concerned, he was a prominent leader of organized crime in Russia; he was a hardened professional thief who was very respected by his colleagues. They have a special title for people like that; he has the special distinction of being what is called a "legal thief." It is a special title, meaning a hardened, high-level criminal. And Ivankov evidently realized that his arrest was imminent, and that is why he chose to attempt to leave Russia. We worked on this particular case together with the FBI. We sent 200 persons here to work on the operation. I hope that the trial in court will be successful in its conclusion.

Senator ROTH. Mr. Minister, some hockey players from the former Soviet Union who play professionally in the United States have become victims of extortion. Is this also a problem in the former Soviet Union, where these players often visit and still have families?

Mr. Kozhevnikov [Interpreted from Russian]. I would not say that our professional athletes are a particular problem inasmuch as on Russian territory, for example. We do have individual incidents, but we do have incidents of extortion not only of athletes, but of a number of persons who have considerable financial wherewithal. But I would not say that this is a particular problem with regard to athletes specifically. That is my opinion, anyway.

Senator ROTH. I will ask you one further question, Mr. Minister. You testified about the theft of radioactive material from facilities in the former Soviet Union. You also testified that this was not material that could be used for manufacturing nuclear weapons. Are there any cases where material or intellectual property, has been stolen or sold, to your knowledge?

Mr. KOZHEVNIKOV [Interpreted from Russian]. Well, we have the federal security system. That is their purview, actually; that is their bailiwick. I am unable to provide you with the appropriate information in that regard because I do not have the facts at hand.

Senator ROTH. Thank you. Senator Lieberman?

Joe Lieberman

Senator LlEBERMAN. Thank you, Mr. Chairman, and thank you, gentlemen from the U.S., and thank you, Minister Kozhevnikov, for the cooperation of the MVD with American law enforcement and for taking the time to be with us this morning.

Let me begin with a general question. In the private sector, when a new business comes in to compete with an existing business, either the market expands, or the existing business goes out of business or diversifies and goes into something else. So here, with a whole new generation of organized criminals and so-called Russian organized crime families or groups coming in, I am wondering what you would say has been the reaction of the existing illegal business groups, the existing organized crime families. Are some of them going into other areas, or do we have a generational change happening where, in a sense, the children now go into legitimate businesses, and that is the end of that operation, or is just the market expanding? Mr. Moody, do you want to start?

Mr. Moody. What we see is that, for instance, the gas tax fraud really started with the American La Cosa Nostra. What we see happening today is that the La Cosa Nostra will basically franchise the operation to the Russian groups and get a kickback in all this, so that everybody makes money. We do not see Russian groups coming in and trying to vie and fight for territory with other organized crime groups. They enter into cooperative agreements. There is enough money out there to be stolen by everybody, and they share the profits.

Senator LIEBERMAN. Mr. Federico or Mr. Weise, does that conform to your perception of what is happening?

Mr. Federico. That conforms exactly to what we have seen. As Mr. Moody said, the Italian mafia, if you will, in New York started the idea of the daisy chain that we described. They then used the abilities of the Russians who had purchased the retail service outlets, and that was a perfect forum for the Russians to get into that. They pay tribute to each other and in fact share the illegal profits.

Mr. Weise. I do not have anything to add to that, Senator.

Senator LIEBERMAN. So the age of mergers has reached illegal activities as well as legal activities in this country, but apparently without the same effects of downsizing that occur in the private sector.

Mr. Federico. It is much more efficient.

Senator Lieberman. It is much more efficient, and the employment opportunities continue to be vigorous.

Mr. Moody. Very much so; they are expanding, not downsizing.

Senator Lieberman. In that regard, I was interested in your testimony, Mr. Weise, about the interception that Customs has done of heroin and other illegal drugs which have been transshipped through the former Soviet Union and the former Warsaw Bloc. First, do you have a sense of how significant a proportion of the drugs coming into the United States are coming through this so- called Russian organized crime network? We tend to think of the drugs coming in most significantly from Latin America, although I know it is more complicated than that.

Mr. Weise. It is difficult to quantify at this point, Senator, but I would say at this point it is very small in terms of total percentage, but it is growing and growing at a fairly fast pace.

Senator Lieberman. Were you tipped off in the case that you described by law enforcement authorities from the former Soviet Union or Warsaw Bloc countries as to the transshipment of illegal drugs, or was that discovered here at point of entry?

Mr. Weise. We have various cases that are working, but that one particular case, we did have some undercover information, and we have had cooperation with other law enforcement organizations in the former Soviet Union.

Bosses meet in the park (Interpol)

Senator Lieberman. And am I correct, hearing your testimony, in saying that the level of that cooperation with law enforcement in the former Soviet Union is going up and is becoming more extensive?

Mr. Weise. Yes.

Senator Lieberman. I wanted to get to a point related to that.
Senator ROTH mentioned in his opening comments that there is not an extradition treaty that now exists between the United States and Russia. I assume that it would be helpful to your efforts, gentlemen, if such a treaty existed. Am I correct in that?

Mr. Moody. Senator, when we first started out, there were no treaties at all. The example Mr. Federico used of the gas tax fraud in Philadelphia, when that case was indicted, there were five individuals who fled back to Eastern Europe. Two of them fled to Russia, two fled to the Ukraine, and I do not know where the fifth one went. At that point, I contacted my counterpart in the MVD and asked him for assistance in Russia to arrest David Shuster and Dmitry Belokopytov, and they did. They arrested for us those two individuals and put them on an airplane flying directly back into the United States, with FBI agents abroad, so that we could then arrest them here in the United States.

At the same time, the two individuals who fled to the Ukraine heard about it, and since the Russian authorities were shot at when they went out to arrest Shuster and Belakopytov, and there was a little physical restraint of these two individuals, well, the two individuals in the Ukraine voluntarily came back.

Alleged member of Russian Organized Crime

Senator Lieberman. They were made an offer they could not refuse.

Mr. Moody. Yes, sir. The Russian authorities did a very good job. When my FBI agent showed up and talked to Mr. Shuster, he said that he was bringing him back to the United States for arrest, and if he gave him any problem, he was going to leave him in Russia; and Shuster's response was, "There will be no problem." From that position, we have gone on, and today, we have a legal agreement that has been signed by Vice President Gore and Vice Premier Chernomyrdin, and we are working toward a mutual legal assistance treaty. I believe that we really need to have that mutual legal assistance treaty which would cover all of this.

Senator Lieberman. So it is not a formal extradition treaty, but there now is a legal agreement that has been achieved at the Gore- Chernomyrden level, and we are moving toward that.

Mr. Moody. Yes, sir.

Senator LlEBERMAN. It is very interesting that the movement of the criminals once identified is not only as it was in the case of Mr. Ivankov that you described from the former Soviet Union here, but also that when indicted here, some of the Russian crime figures have gone back there. So it is obviously important that we have mutual extradition.
I did want to ask both Mr. Kozhevnikov and the others, in the case of Mr. Ivankov, did you know when he was heading to the United States? Were you able to track him at that time? And then I want to ask the Americans here how did he gain entry into the United States?

Alleged member of Russian Organized Crime

Mr. Moody. If I may add. Senator, we are not exactly sure how he gained entry into the United States. The Russian authorities told us he was coming and that he came into the United States. We are not exactly sure. We know he went in and out of the United States a number of times. The Russian authorities told us about him and basically where he was located and enabled us to start targeting him for investigation, which ultimately led, with their cooperation, to his indictment. I believe he goes on trial this month.

When we arrested him, I believe we found him with seven different passports in seven different names. That gives you some idea of what we are facing internationally today with the rapid communication systems, with the rapid ability to travel inter nationally, and with the counterfeiting — or a lot of these passports are legitimate passports in a number of different names — it is very difficult to keep up with these individuals.

Senator ROTH. Were they all phony passports, or were they bona fide?

Mr. Moody. Some of them were legitimate with different names.

Senator Lieberman. So that in other words, they are unlikely to be coming in under their real names. I am wondering to what extent it would help if in this cooperative relationship you have with the Russian authorities — well, the immigration officials, for instance, had a list of the names of organized Russian crime families

Mr. Moody. We have received lists of names from the Russian authorities and have provided them to Immigration to help keep these individuals out. We have also provided them to the State Department as a screening mechanism.

Senator LIEBERMAN. Has that had any effect in the sense of apprehending any of them, or are they coming in mostly under assumed names?

Mr. Moody. If I may, it has had more of a deterrent effect; it makes it a little more difficult for them to come in. And there are certain very well-known individuals who are trying to come into the United States who have been barred from coming into the United States.

Senator Lieberman. Very well-known as organized crime figures in Russia?

Mr. Moody. Yes, sir.

Senator LIEBERMAN. And again, are they attempting to come in to escape prosecution in Russia, or are they just coming in because it is better business? Mr. Kozhevnikov?

Mr. Kozhevnikov [Interpreted from Russian] . I can say that you are correct when you speak about the need to exchange more information. I have in mind information which each side has at its disposal. We are working with the FBI just now to prepare a list of persons who, in our view, are planning to move to the United States to engage in criminal activity, and we intend to hand it over in the near future. But we would like also to get similar information on former citizens who are already here now and have been convicted so that we might be able to use this information for our own purposes. On the whole, I would say we are moving in the direction of closer cooperation.

Senator LIEBERMAN. That is good news for both sides, and I hope it will continue. May I ask you this question, and you alluded to it in your testimony. There has been a general impression given that Russian organized crime figures here in this country are not operating, at least at this point, in a tightly-structured organization, that there are more individual illegal entrepreneurs! Do you have any evidence that the Russian criminal figures are sending members of their groups over here to go into this, and are there continuing relations, economic or otherwise, between the crime families in Russia and those Russian organized crime figures here, or is it totally a separate, independent operation in the United States?

Mr. Kozhevnikov [Interpreted from Russian]. We were speaking of well-known criminal families — I missed the beginning of that; I did not hear the soundtrack.

Senator LIEBERMAN. Unfortunately, the translation was not working earlier. Let me just ask the basic question again very briefly. Is there a connection between organized crime families in Russia and those that operate here in the United States?

Mr. Kozhevnikov [Interpreted from Russian]. We have at our disposal preliminary intelligence to the effect that such contacts are taking place.

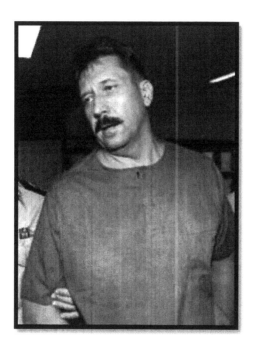

Viktor Anatoliyevich Bout

Senator LIEBERMAN. Thank you. I have a final question for the gentlemen from U.S. law enforcement. As to the violence that is being committed by members of Russian organized crime, is it as we have become accustomed to experiencing with earlier groups, primarily within the groups themselves fighting for turf, or is violence used against nonmembers. against the targets of extortion or other criminal activities by Russian organized crime in the United States?

Mr. Moody. We see the use of both. In a case out of Philadelphia, I believe, 10 Russians were killed. They were killing each other during that investigation. But we also see in the Ivankov investigation that the father of one of the victims was beaten to death on a subway platform in Moscow. We see both the use of violence — they very readily use violence, and they very readily use violence against law enforcement.

Mr. Federico. That is a trait that I think we have to respect and guard against, their willingness to use violence against law enforcement.

Senator LlEBERMAN. Including in the United States?

Mr. Moody. I do not know of any specific example in the United States yet. We have picked up intelligence information that it is being considered.

Senator LlEBERMAN. But they have employed violence against law enforcement within Russia.

Mr. Moody. Within Russia, it is a very significant problem, and maybe he will tell you about it — the number of law enforcement officials who have been killed in the last few years.

Senator LlEBERMAN. Am I correct that that traditionally has not been a pattern of organized crime?

Mr. Moody. In the United States.

Senator LlEBERMAN. Yes, in the United States, that they have not used violence against law enforcement for fear of reprisals, I presume.

Zakhar Knyazevich Kalashov, the alleged head of the Georgian mafia

Mr. Moody. That is correct; in the United States, they have not.

Senator LIEBERMAN. So that if these intelligence reports are correct, it would be a new and, to put it mildly, unsettling, outrageous development here.

Mr. Moody. Yes, sir. We have had discussions with certain of these individuals about the down sides of doing something like that.

Senator LIEBERMAN. So you have actually had informal but direct warnings?

Mr. Moody. Yes, sir. We have had the same thing over the years with the La Cosa Nostra.

Senator LlEBERMAN. Thank you for what you are doing. I wish you well. Thank you, Mr. Chairman.

Senator ROTH. Thank you. Senator Cohen?

Senator Cohen. Thank you, Mr. Chairman. I know this panel has been going on for some time, and we want to release them so we can get to the other panels, but I would just like to pose a couple of thoughts.

Since I have served on this Subcommittee, we have investigated a variety of issues involving organized crime. We have investigated, for example, the organization of "chop shops" in the United States, money laundering operations, currency exchange operators along our borders, professional boxing, a whole variety of areas. We have found a commonality of issues involved in each of these cases. Number one, there are big profits involved. Whenever there are big profits, and on the other side of the equation, you have low risk — low risk of detection, low risk of prosecution, low risk of conviction and low risk of sentencing — you are going to have a proliferation of activity in this particular field. We have found it in virtually every area we have ever investigated.

What comes to mind as I listened to the testimony this morning is that we have precisely the same situation here. There is a very low rate of detection — I think you indicated, Mr. Weise, that but for the agent sitting behind you and his picking up one small piece of information, that business of Electrodyne exporting the blue- prints never would have been detected.

That raises several issues in my mind. First of all, on the first chart you showed, you indicated that there were 6,000 grams of heroin being smuggled in, and you said that 14 people have been convicted. My question is what were the sentences given out to those 14 individuals who were convicted?

Mr. Weise. We will get you that specifically for the record, Senator, but I am being informed that it was consistent with the Federal guidelines on each of those kinds of cases; but we will get you that specifically. But your point is well-taken, that probably one might say it was not severe enough.

Senator COHEN. Well, whether we are talking about heroin smuggling, auto theft, military equipment coming back into the United States, the question is what are the chances of it being detected, successfully prosecuted, and if prosecuted successfully, what is the sentence going to be? I raise this in connection with Mr. Kozhevnikov, and I will turn to him in a moment, but I read the memoirs of Natan Sharansky. I assume that the prison conditions and sentences in Mother Russia are not exactly "Club Fed," or maybe in this case. Club Med, but in any event, I assume that the authorities in Russia do not have Federal courts which oversee the living conditions, the number of people who serve in their particular prisons, whether or not their living conditions are up to standards as far as Federal standards are concerned.

In other words, we have a situation where you have people who are leaving, organized crime figures who leave Russia to come here, with little prospect of being caught, detected, convicted, and then sentenced to what — something that is quite easy, I would assume, by Russian standards. As I go back and read Sharansky's memoirs being put away, is not exactly a holiday.

So I raise this as an issue because it seems to me — and you have indicated, Mr. Moody, that this is in the initial stages. What is going to stop this tide from expanding if in fact they keep looking at the profit side, with the low risk of detection and prosecution, and then what is the penalty going to be?

I think it is probably not feasible, but one might propose that if we have these international links that have been established, as Senator Lieberman was talking about, between organized Russian gangs here and the gangs back home, perhaps we might have a policy of extradition, and if we in fact apprehend people who are violating our laws, and they do have connections back to the homeland, that we send them there for prosecution and conviction and sentencing. That might be a greater disincentive than we currently have under our own rules.

Mr. Weise, you got my attention in terms of Electrodyne sending out these blueprints basically to subcontract to manufacture certain component parts that go into our military equipment. We have all been fixated, and justifiably so, on the recent tragedy that occurred with one of our commercial airliners going down. We have had evidence, for example, that suspected unapproved parts are making their way back into the commercial airline industry, that is cause for concern to all of us. But if you think about the implications of allowing parts to our military equipment being factored out or subcontracted out, coming back in, it would seem to me to make logical sense for a foreign military or intelligence operation to in fact encourage organized criminal groups to be manufactured parts to come back into the United States to go into our military equipment.

It would seem to me you would have a perfect marriage between officials of another government cooperating with organized criminal elements to achieve precisely the placing of defective or inferior parts in your potential adversaries' military equipment.

Mr. Weise. Senator, that is precisely the reason why we included that example in our testimony notwithstanding the fact that we do not have direct evidence of whether or not it is

Senator COHEN. But it raises another issue as to what we can do about it. For example, is there any law that would prohibit a major military contractor in the United States from contracting out the manufacture of certain component parts to established allies? We know, for example, that when we talk about an American-made car, the engine might come from Canada, the body might come from Mexico, the electronics might come from Japan.

Now, we are talking about a multinational defense contractor. Is there any prohibition — you are going to be advised there in a moment — is there any prohibition on these multinational contractors from having any of the parts made in other countries that are allies of ours?

Mr. Weise. Well, clearly. Senator, you are getting well beyond our area of expertise, and yet what is being whispered to me is that there are Department of Defense guidelines, which obviously the Department of Defense would be much more appropriate to be answering these questions.

Senator COHEN. Then, my follow-up question would be do you have any kind of a liaison relationship with the Department of Defense to coordinate your investigations with DOD. Are you able to determine whether or not, if it is permissible — we have what we call "false flag" operations in the business, an ally could be manufacturing a component part for a piece of defense equipment which in turn has been compromised because that particular operation is really being run by another organization by another country.

Mr. Weise. And the answer to your question is we clearly consulted very closely with the Department of Defense, both on these matters and all of our export control responsibilities.

Senator COHEN. OK. Mr. Kozhevnikov, how many police have been murdered in Russia in the last year or so? Is it roughly 500?

Mr. Kozhevnikov [Interpreted from Russian]. I think I can give you the exact number; about 278 in 1995. These are persons who were involved in performing their formal obligation.

Senator COHEN. And do you have any evidence of Russian political figures being either extorted, intimidated or otherwise compromised by organized crime groups in Russia?

Mr. Kozhevnikov [Interpreted from Russian]. Well, if we want to speak about well-known political figures, we do not have such data or information. If we want to speak about local authorities, yes, we can confirm that such instances do take place.

Senator COHEN. We know that organized Chechen groups that operate in southern Russia are involved in a produce inventory operation. Do you know whether any of the Chechen organized groups operate in the United States?

Mr. Kozhevnikov [Interpreted from Russian]. I have no information on Chechens in the United States.

Senator Cohen. Thank you. Thank you very much, Mr. Chairman. I know you are anxious to move on.

Mr. Moody. Senator, we have arrested Chechens in the United States.

Senator ROTH. Thank you. Thank you, Senator Cohen, and thank you, gentlemen, very much. We appreciate your very helpful and informative testimony. Mr. Minister, thank you again for being here. At this time, I would like to call forward our next witness, Michael Franzese, a former captain in the Colombo organized crime family. Mr. Franzese, as you know, we swear in all witnesses who appear before this Subcommittee, so would you please rise and raise your right hand?

Mr. Franzese. Yes.

Senator ROTH. Do you swear or affirm that the testimony you will give to this Subcommittee will be the truth, the whole truth, and nothing but the truth, so help you, God?

Mr. Franzese. I do.

Senator ROTH. Thank you, and please proceed with your testimony.

TESTIMONY OF MICHAEL FRANZESE, FORMER CAPO, COLOMBO ORGANIZED CRIME FAMILY

Mr. Franzese. Good morning, distinguished Members of the Subcommittee. My name is Michael Franzese, and I have been subpoenaed here today to address the Subcommittee regarding my personal experiences with Russian organized crime in the United States. I order to understand the extent of that activity, the

Subcommittee needs to be aware of my own background and former involvement in organized crime.

I was born in Brooklyn, New York. My father is John "Sonny" Franzese, former underboss of the Colombo crime family, one of New York's five La Cosa Nostra families. In 1975, I became a "made" member of the Colombo family, in a formal induction ceremony presided over by then family boss, Thomas DiBella.

I acted in the capacity of "soldier" from 1975 through 1980, when I was appointed a "Caporegime" and given a crew of soldiers to preside over.

During the years I was a member, I engaged in criminal activity on my own behalf as well as that of the Colombo family, such criminal activity included tax fraud loan sharking, gambling, securities fraud, labor racketeering and extortion.

In 1985, I was indicted in the Eastern District of New York for various racketeering charges. In 1986, as part of a plea agreement with the Organized Crime Strike Force of the Department of Justice, I pled guilty to 2 counts of the 28-count indictment relating to tax fraud. I accepted a 10-year prison sentence and $15 million in fines and restitution.

In or about 1987, while in Federal prison in California, I decided to sever my 12-year relationship with the Colombo crime family and organized crime in general. As I address the Subcommittee here today, I am no longer a member of organized crime.

In early 1980, while I was a Colombo family soldier, Lawrence Iorizzo, a major independent gasoline wholesaler based in Long Island, New York, came to me for protection. Iorizzo and Russian organized crime figures working independently of one another each figured out how to orchestrate one of the most lucrative Government rip-offs of all time — stealing gas tax money.

As you have been told by previous witnesses, this was a complex scam that, over the years, has netted Italian and Russian organized crime hundreds and hundreds of millions of dollars. And the Russians pioneered and perfected these schemes to where I understand it is still going on today despite changes in the law.

I first got involved because some mob figures were trying to shake down Iorizzo. Iorizzo owned or operated some 300 independent gas stations throughout Long Island at that time. It was a cash-heavy operation. I resolved Iorizzo's problem by sending some of my men over to let these other mob figures know Iorizzo was with me. That ended Iorizzo's problem. In return, I became his partner in the wholesale gasoline business, and this business be- came an organized crime-controlled operation.

Later in 1980, I began working with Russians in the gas tax business. One of my soldiers, a guy named Vinnie, had been approached by the Russians to help collect a $70,000 debt. Vinnie's job was to say, "Pay the money, or I'll break your legs," and to sound convincing, which he was. My guy came to me with the Russian's offer to see if I was interested. I was, and so I arranged a meeting with the leaders of this Russian organized crime group — Michael Markowitz, David Bogatin, and Lev Persits. These men owned and operated a wholesale gasoline company in Brooklyn, New York.

These Russians were having trouble collecting money owned them. They were also having problems obtaining and holding onto the licenses they needed to keep the gas tax scam going. I could help them on both counts. First, the Colombo family's reputation was very effective in causing people to pay their debts. Also, our family had a guy at the commissioner of revenue's office at the State House in Albany who could get the necessary licenses.

The Russians were eager to align themselves with someone who could resolve both problems. Because of my association with organized crime, they believed me to be that person. As it turned out, I was.

We arranged a sit-down on a Saturday morning in the fall of 1980 at a Mobil station they owned in Brooklyn. The three Russians told me how they were stealing tax money due the Government on the sale of gasoline and how they often ran into problems collecting some of the illegal proceeds from their customers.

We cut a deal whereby they agreed to become part of my organization. I would provide them with protection from the other mob families and the muscle to collect all the money due them. Through the services of Lawrence Iorizzo and our gasoline operation, they would have access to the wholesale licenses they needed to defraud the State, county, and Federal Government out of tax revenue.

We agreed to share the illegal proceeds, 75 percent my end, 25 percent their end. The deal was put on record with all five crime families, and I took care of the Colombo family share out of the illegal proceeds of my end.

Over the next 4 years, the combined Russian-Iorizzo organization which I controlled defrauded the United States Government and the States and counties of New York, Connecticut, New Jersey, Pennsylvania and Florida out of hundreds of millions of tax dollars due on the sale of gasoline.

To give you an idea how lucrative the gas tax business was, it was not unusual for me to receive $9 million in cash per week in paper bags from the Russians and Iorizzo. Our profits ran any- where from 2 to 30 cents per gallon, and at one point, we were moving 400 to 500 million gallons per month. I will leave it to you to do the math.

During that time, I became very closely involved with the Russian group. I found them to be intelligent, possessing remarkable business instincts that they would not hesitate to use for illegal gain. As a result of their experiences living in Communist Russia, they have little respect for United States law and little fear of American prisons.

They would frequently approach me with other illegal business ventures and were eager to share in illegal deals I would propose to them, such as loan sharking, insurance fraud and securities fraud.

One of the business ventures we jointly entered into was budding a bank in Austria. The purpose of this transaction was to be able to use this bank to finance other organized crime ventures. I in- vested $10 million from my end of the illegal gas tax profits in this bank.

Including the money invested by the Russians, the bank had a total of $80 to $100 million in assets. Bogatin later went to Austria, where he played an active role in operating this bank. Additionally, lorizzo created a slush fund from Federal gas tax money, which he kept in this Austrian bank. That account accumulated $15 million when the Government seized it after lorizzo's arrest.

I found the Russians to be a group that wanted to flex their muscles and would not hesitate to resort to violence when they felt it necessary to do so. They enjoyed the relationship with both myself and the Colombo family because it gave them power and recognition as a group to be reckoned with.

I did not find the Russian criminals to be a very structured group in comparison to the Italian La Cosa Nostra. They were very clannish, however, and the most financially successful Russian was looked up to by his comrades as their leader or boss. The boss was given a lot of courtesy and respect and in return provided the members of his group with opportunities to work for him and make money.

Michael Markowitz, David Bogatin and Lev Persits were all in a position of leadership and had about 200 other Russians working under them in various capacities. They were also continuously assisting other Russians in immigrating to the United States.

After I went to prison in 1985, my information was that Markowitz, Bogatin and Persits did continue to work with the Colombo family in the gasoline business for a short period of time.

Around 1988, Markowitz was shot and killed in front of his home in Brooklyn. I do not know who was responsible for his death. How- ever, I am reasonably certain that the hit was authorized by the Colombo family and could possibly have been carried out by other Russians.

An attempt was also made on the life of Lev Persits. Although he survived the attempt, he is permanently disabled and confined to a wheelchair today.

David Bogatin fled to Austria, where he had a controlling inter- est in the bank that was funded with gasoline tax money from our operation. He was captured in Poland, extradited to the United States to face tax fraud charges and is currently serving a Federal prison sentence.

I have provided the Subcommittee with a basic overview of my personal experience with Russian immigrants engaging in criminal activities during the 1980s. I hope this information is helpful, and I would be happy to answer any questions the Subcommittee might have. Thank you.

Senator ROTH. Thank you, Mr. Franzese. You stated that in your opinion, these fraudulent measures with the fuel tax continue. Does it continue on as large a scale as in the past?

Mr. Franzese. I do not believe so. I believe that once the law was changed, the volume and the methods decreased. But I am told — I was recently released from prison in 1994, and I met several people who had still been dealing with the Russians, and I am told that especially in New York, the gas tax scheme was continuing as late as 1994.

Senator ROTH. And on a fairly large scale?

Mr. Franzese. Yes, on a large scale, but not quite as large as it was in the 1980s.

Senator ROTH. At the peak of your gas tax business, how many gas stations were involved?

Mr. Franzese. I would say well over 600 stations, and it could have been close to 1,000 gas stations that we operated or sold gas to.

Senator ROTH. And how many of those were brand name stations?

Mr. Franzese. Approximately a third.

Senator ROTH. How were you first introduced to the Russians?

Mr. Franzese. I met the Russians through a soldier in my organization. The Russians had gone to him, asking if he could help them collect a debt. They were owed $70,000. This fellow, whose name was Vinnie, came to me and asked my permission to assist the Russians, and I told him he could do it. At that point, they asked to meet me personally, and a meeting was set up.

Senator ROTH. Now, you testified that you provided the Russians with protection from other organized crime families and muscle to collect their debts. What exactly did you do in each of these areas?

Mr. Franzese. Well, as far as collecting the debts, I just made sure that any gasoline stations or other wholesalers that they serviced would pay the money that was due them. And as far as protecting them from other organized crime groups, I put them on record with every other family that they were with me and part of my operation and that no one else was to try to muscle in on them or try to do business with them.

Senator ROTH. If the Russians brought this business to you, how did you come to the decision that there would be a 75-25 percent split?

Mr. Franzese. I explained to them that we were taking most of the risk, we were securing the license, and that I had to take care of the rest of the Colombo family and, quite honestly, I knew that to a large degree, they controlled some of the money, and there was a lot of stealing going on amongst each other. So I just rounded it off to 75-25 percent, and they were satisfied with that.

Senator ROTH. Out of the 75 percent you took, how much did you keep and how much went to the Colombo family?

Mr. Franzese. About one-third went to the Colombo family. The other two-thirds was split among myself and the various people that I had working in the operation.

Senator ROTH. Since Markowitz was such a big money-maker for you and the Colombo family, why was he killed?

Mr. Franzese. I believe for two reasons. Number one, he was reluctant to work with the rest of the Colombo family once I went to prison. And I also understand that he might have been cooperating with Federal authorities.

Senator ROTH. Do you have any insights as to how Russian organized crime is developing in this country? Do you have any knowledge as to how they are cooperating with more traditional, established organized crime families?

Mr. Franzese. I could only speak of my own experience, that they were very willing to cooperate with our group. La Cosa Nostra. They were not interested in trying to fight with us; they would rather share proceeds. They had no problem with working along with us. And from my understanding, they are continuing to operate in that way today.

Senator ROTH. Senator Cohen?

Senator COHEN. Had the Colombo family not thought of the fuel tax scam previously, before the Russians arrived?

Mr. Franzese. The Colombo family had not. I actually introduced this to the Colombo family when Iorizzo came to me originally, and we had developed this scheme, and to my surprise, I found out the Russians were also doing it when I met them; they just did not have the muscle to collect their money, and they did not have the availability of the licenses that were needed.

Senator COHEN. I am just curious as to why you would want to share any part of the market with anyone. In other words, you have an established organized criminal group; why would you want to share on a 75-25 or 50-50 or any percentage basis? If you have an idea, and you have the organization, and you have the muscle yourself, why would you want to let another group come in and take a portion of it?

Mr. Franzese. Well, the way the transaction worked, the Russians had about 300 stations themselves that they were supplying. So by allowing them to write off on our license, we obtained proceeds from those 300 stations that we would not ordinarily have had.

Senator Cohen. In other words, they were already in the business, and this was just a pure business decision to share the wealth at that particular point.

Mr. Franzese. Yes.

Senator COHEN. But if I were to come up now as a result of listening to your testimony and others, and say, "Hey, I've got a great idea of how to scam the Government," would I find resistance from organized criminal elements to my entering the marketplace?

Mr. Franzese. I do not believe so. If you brought profit to the table, I do not believe there would be any resistance at all.

Senator Cohen. If I have an idea, and I do not have the muscle, they would be willing to allow me to enter the marketplace?

Mr. Franzese. I believe so, yes.

Senator COHEN. So there was no fear on the part of the existing organized criminal groups that they would have to deal with the violent element in the Russian gangs; was that not a factor?

Mr. Franzese. There was no fear at all from La Cosa Nostra, no. They were not worried about that. I found the Russians to be actually kind of submissive to us. Although I found they would not hesitate to be violent amongst each other, I thought that they were really worried about us, and I thought they were fearful of us as a group, and therefore they would rather align with us than fight with us.

Senator COHEN. You also indicated that the Russians have no fear of our laws as such; right?

Mr. Franzese. Yes. They indicated to me that Russian prisons were hell and that the prisons here in America were like clubs, and the laws in Russia were very strict. As a matter of fact, I know Bogatin had done some time, and I think both Markowitz and Persits had experienced Russian prisons. So they had no fear whatsoever of the law or the prison system here.

Senator Cohen. And that would continue to be the case today, then?

Mr. Franzese. I believe so. I do not know why it would change so dramatically.

Senator Cohen. What might be hard time for you might not be hard time for someone else.

Mr. Franzese. According to them, that is correct.

Senator Cohen. Do you know whether they are tied to other organized criminal groups of the Sicilians, the Colombians? Are they engaging in narcotics traffic in cooperation with other existing groups?

Mr. Franzese. I do not know that from my own personal knowledge, no.

Senator COHEN. Do you know whether the new Russian organized criminal elements coming into the United States are more violent than the existing ones?

Mr. Franzese. I am hearing that they are more violent, yes.

Senator COHEN. And also more sophisticated in terms of their capabilities?

Mr. Franzese. Well, I thought the group that I was with was very sophisticated. Markowitz had several educational degrees. He was an engineer. He had developed a taxi meter, a computerized meter, that I think was first introduced in New York. I found them to be very intelligent even at that time.

Senator Cohen. I was going to bring this out in the previous panel, but my understanding is that the FBI is looking for a few good men and women, particularly with backgrounds in math and computer science, in order to combat the sophistication of the crime groups that are coming in.

Mr. Franzese. Yes.

Senator Cohen. And I guess we are going to have to do that for the IRS and the FBI and all the other elements involved, because as criminal groups become more sophisticated, as they move into cyberspace, as they are able to engage in computer hacking, allowing them to access the vaults of various banks here in the United States and worldwide and with a stroke of a key on a computer, funnel off millions of dollars in a matter of seconds, we are going to need more sophisticated methods of combating these criminals. So that is something that I think we also have to focus on.

Mr. Franzese. Yes, sir. One other thing that I noticed is that when the Government changed the gasoline law and they made the responsibility of collecting taxes, they shifted it from the retailer at the gas station level to the wholesaler, and they thought they were going to put everybody out of business. But what I found is that they advertised the fact that they were going to do that over several months — they made it public — and by the time they changed the law, we had a perfected scheme that made it even more lucrative than the one we had before. So I think maybe some kind of concealment in that regard might be helpful.

Senator COHEN. Do you think we can pass laws in a concealed, covert fashion?

Mr. Franzese. I do not know. I do not know.

Senator Cohen. I think I have already answered the question.

Mr. Franzese. Yes.

Senator Cohen. Thank you, Mr. Chairman.

Senator ROTH. Thank you. Senator Cohen. That will be all Mr. Franzese. Thank you.

Mr. Franzese. Thank you.

Senator ROTH. Our next witness is Anthony Casso, who is a former underboss of the Lucchese organized crime family. Mr. Casso is currently in Federal custody and cooperating with the Government while awaiting sentencing.
Given the sensitive nature of Mr. Casso's position as a cooperating witness, we have agreed to limit his testimony to matters relating to Russian organized crime, and we would appreciate the cooperation of all Subcommittee members in abiding by this understanding.
Mr. Casso was scheduled to testify openly; however, as a result of last-minute concerns raised by the Department of Justice, Mr. Casso will testify from behind a screen. It is my understanding that members of the media have already been

advised as to those locations in the hearing room where cameras will and will not be permitted during the course of the testimony in order to maintain security.

Prior to the entrance of this witness, I direct that all cameras be turned to face either to the ceiling or to the window side of the hearing room. I will ask the Capitol Police whether all cameras have been redirected. And I would then ask the Capitol Police to secure the hearing room, and when that is done, the witness will be brought in.

We will proceed in just a minute.

Mr. Casso, we swear all witnesses before the Subcommittee, but I would ask that you remain seated while I administer the oath.

Mr. Casso, please raise your right hand. Do you swear or affirm that the testimony you will give before this Subcommittee is the truth, the whole truth, and nothing but the truth, so help you, God?

Mr. Casso: I do.

Senator ROTH. Mr. Casso, are you represented by counsel today, and if so, would counsel please identify yourself and your firm for the record.

Mr. Brief. Matthew Brief, B-r-i-e-f, Brief, Kesselman, Knapp and Schulman.

Senator ROTH. Mr. Casso, would you please proceed with your testimony?

Alleged Russian Mafia member Dmitri "Dimmy" Belrov known associate of Nikolay Radev,

TESTIMONY OF ANTHONY CASSO, FORMER UNDERBOSS, LUCCHESE ORGANIZED CRIME FAMILY, ACCOMPANIED BY MATTHEW BRIEF, LAW FIRM OF BRIEF, KESSELMAN, KNAPP AND SCHULMAN

Mr. Casso. Good afternoon, Mr. Chairman and Members of the Subcommittee. My name is Anthony Casso. Early in my life, I was given the nickname of "Gaspipe."

I have been in jail since 1993, when I was arrested after being a fugitive for almost 3 years. At that time, I was the underboss of the Lucchese organized crime family. Ultimately, I decided to cooperate rather than go to trial.

As part of my deal with the Government, I pleaded guilty to a 72-count indictment, including murder, racketeering and extortion. I have not yet been sentenced, and no promises have been made to me for my testimony here today. As part of my cooperation agreement, I told the Government about my life of crime. I gave a deposition for use in an Israeli trial, but I have not yet testified at a trial in the United States. I will testify if requested by the Government at upcoming organized crime trials.

I have been involved with organized crime for more than 35 years, since I was a kid working on the docks in Brooklyn, New York. When I was 21, I became associated with a guy named Chris Furnari of the Lucchese organized crime family. Everyone knows him as "Christy Tick."

Before I was arrested this time, I had only been in jail once. That was in 1962 for 5 days, when I was convicted of running a book- making operation on the docks and was fined $50. After that, I was arrested several times for different Federal and State charges including assault with a gun, selling stolen property, dealing heroin, burglarizing a bank, and bribing State parole officers. In every case, I was either acquitted, or the charges were dropped.

Casso

In the early 1970s, I met Vic Amuso. Then, in 1974, I became a "made" member of the Lucchese family. Vic was "made" in around 1977. At that time, "Tony Ducks" Corallo was the boss of our family. But in 1986, Tony Ducks went to jail, so he had to name a new boss. I became a "capo" in 1986.

After discussions within the family, Tony Ducks made Vic Amuso the boss at the end of 1986. At the end of 1987, Vic told me I was the new Consiglieri. Then, in 1989, Vic named me the underboss of the family. After Vic was arrested in July 1991, I ran the Lucchese family as underboss while I was a fugitive.

In my position as a member of the Lucchese family, I came to know individuals associated with Russian organized crime, which is the subject I have been asked to testify about today.

In the mid-1980s, our family got involved with Russian organized crime in the gasoline business in Brooklyn. Italian and Russian organized crime made large amounts of money by working scams to avoid paying taxes on gasoline. The Russians owned hundreds of gas stations and controlled the supply and distribution of gasoline. We provided them with protection they needed to maintain a cartel. We also helped them set up corporations to work the scam.

The main Russian guy working with our family was Marat Balagula. Marat was one of the early leaders of Russian organized crime in Brooklyn. He made millions off the gas tax business, and our family made a lot of money with him.

Marat Balagula

In around late 1986, another Russian named Vladimir, whose last name I did not know at the time, came up to Marat in a Russian restaurant in Brighton Beach. Vladimir had recently arrived in Brighton Beach from Russia. According to the Russians, the word on the street was that he was a tough guy with his own crew. Marat told me Vladimir pulled a gun, put it next to Marat's head, told Marat that he was his new partner, and demanded Marat pay him $600,000, or Marat would be dead. Marat reached out to us and told us what happened. We agreed to meet him the next day. When we went to Marat's house, we found out that he was so scared that he had a heart attack but did not want to go to the hospital. I remember seeing Marat in bed, hooked up to all kinds of machines, refusing his doctor's orders to go to the hospital. Marat's guy wanted us to kill Vladimir.

Since Marat was with our family, and especially since he was such a moneymaker for us, this was not just a threat against Marat; this was a threat against the Lucchese family as well. We knew what we had to do.

Vic and I agreed that Vladimir had to be killed. We took this situation to Christy Tick, who agreed that we could have Vladimir killed. Vic gave the hit to Joey Testa.

Otar "Otty" Vyachaslav alleged Russian hitman

We asked Marat and one of his guys to get us some information to identify Vladimir. One of Marat's guys got us his picture and license plate number. We had Marat call Vladimir and arrange to have lunch with him at the same Russian restaurant in Brighton Beach where Marat was threatened. After leaving the restaurant, Vladimir was shot and killed.

I heard about the murder on the radio. Marat was very thankful that we had gotten rid of this problem. We could not let somebody try to put the squeeze on one of our family's biggest moneymakers. After that, Marat did not have any more problems from any other Russians.

I found the Russian organized crime groups to be very clever. We knew the Russians were involved in heroin trafficking as well as complicated scams involving forgery, and tax evasion in the oil and gas business. The Russians were also very willing to use violence to achieve their goals.

I will be happy to answer any questions you have about my knowledge of Russian organized crime.

Senator ROTH. Mr. Casso, at this time, do you know the man you identified in your statement as "Vladimir" to be Vladimir Reznikov?

NOTE ON THE TEXT: Vladimir Reznikov (d. June 13, 1986, Brighton Beach, Brooklyn, New York City) was a Russian American gangster. After attempting to extort money from rival gangster Marat Balagula, Reznikov was shot dead by the Lucchese crime family, to whom Balagula was paying street tax. Reznikov's murder remained unsolved until the 1994 cooperation of Lucchese acting boss Anthony Casso. According to Casso, the shooting was actually committed by Joseph Testa and Anthony Senter, two veterans of the DeMeo crew. In the spring of 1986, the Colombo crime family crew led by Michael Franzese began shaking down associates of Balagula, who was running a multi-billion dollar gasoline bootlegging operation. In response, Balagula asked for a sit-down with Christopher Furnari, the Consiglieri for the Lucchese crime family. After the sit-down took place in Brooklyn's 19th Hole social club, Balgula agreed to pay street tax to the Lucchese family. The money was not only strategically shared, but also became the Five Families' biggest moneymaker after narcotics trafficking. According to Philip Carlo, "It didn't take long for word on the street to reach the Russian underworld: Marat Balagula was paying off the Italians; Balagula was a punk; Balagula had no balls. Balagula's days were numbered. This, of course, was the beginning of serious trouble. Balagula did in fact have balls -- he was a ruthless killer when necessary -- but he also was a smart diplomatic administrator and he knew that the combined, concerted force of the Italian crime families would quickly wipe the newly arrived Russian competition off the proverbial map." Shortly afterward, on June 12, 1986, Vladimir Reznikov entered Balagula's headquarters at the Rasputin nightclub. He pushed a 9mm Beretta into Balagula's skull and demanded $600,000 as the price of not pulling the trigger. He also demanded a percentage of everything Balagula was involved in. After Balagula promised to get the money, Reznikov snarled, "Fuck with me and you're dead -- you and your whole fucking family; I swear I'll fuck and kill your wife as you watch -- you understand?" Shortly after Reznikov left, Balagula suffered a massive heart attack. He insisted, however on being treated at his home in Brighton Beach, where he felt it would be harder for Reznikov to kill him. When Lucchese underboss Anthony Casso arrived, he listened to what had happened and said, "Send word to Vladimir that you have his money, that he should come to the club tomorrow. We'll take care of the rest." Casso also requested a photograph of Reznikov and a description of his car. The following day, Reznikov arrived at Balagula's nightclub to pick up his money. Instead, Reznikov was confronted by Gambino associate Joseph Testa, who fatally shot him on Casso's orders. According to Casso, "After that, Marat didn't have any problems with other Russians."

Mr. Casso. Yes, I do.

Senator ROTH. And in addition to the murder you just described in previous testimony, we have also been told of another murder in Brooklyn of a Russian organized crime figure who worked with La Cosa Nostra in the gas tax scam, that is, the killing of Michael Markowitz who worked with the Colombo family. What were the facts surrounding this murder, and describe any discussions you had with anyone in the Colombo family regarding the Markowitz murder?

Mr. Casso. I had discussions with the Colombo boss, Vic Orena and a Colombo soldier, Frankie "The Bug" Sciortino.

Senator ROTH. Would you please speak into the microphone?

Mr. Casso. And I knew the Markowitz murder was going to take place sooner or later, that they were working on planning on killing Markowitz.

Mob wedding

Senator ROTH. Now, you testified that the Lucchese family provided protection to Russian organized crime in the gas tax scheme. Specifically, what protection service did your family provide for the Russians?

Mr. Casso. We provided that no one would go into their territory and sell gas, and made sure people paid them the moneys they had coming to them. And we would make it known that they belonged with us, our group, and no one would bother them at all.

Senator ROTH. Now, you testified that Marat Balagula was a leading figure among Russian organized crime in Brooklyn. Why would he contact you after he was threatened by another Russian?

Marat Balagula

Mr. Casso. Because Marat was with our family, so the proper thing to do was just what he did, to contact us to handle it.

Senator ROTH. Where is Balagula today?

Mr. Casso. He is in Federal prison, I believe.

Senator ROTH. Did Balagula actually ask you to have Reznikov killed, or simply to make him back off?

Mr. Casso. No; he wanted him killed. He was deathly afraid of him.

Senator ROTH. Did you receive any payment for killing Reznikov?

Mr. Casso. None whatsoever.

Senator ROTH. Was Joey Testa given any payment for killing Reznikov?

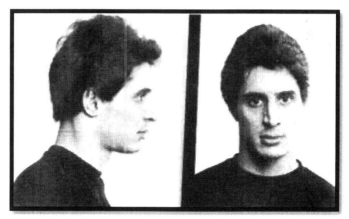

Joey Testa, known shooter and Anthony Senter. Senter and Testa, better known the Gemini twins are two mobsters in the Lucchese crime family. Senter and Testa are former members of the DeMeo crew in the Gambino crime family. In 1989, both Senter and Testa were found guilty of racketeering and 10 counts of murder and both were sentenced to life in federal prison. Anthony Michael Senter was born in Canarsie, Brooklyn, New York to immigrants Michael Senter and wife from Rovereto, Italy. Senter's uncle, Gambino and Colombo associate, Robert Senter owned the Canarsie Recycling Company in Canarsie. As a young man Anthony worked at both his father's small debris removal business and his uncle's sanitation company. Robert Senter gained notoriety for the kidnapping and murder of Emanuel Gambino, the nephew of Gambino crime family boss Carlo Gambino and nephew of Paul Castellano. On December 4, 1972, Robert Senter was arrested and confessed to the murder of Gambino. He also revealed the identities of Richard Chaisson and Warren Schurman who were his two accomplices. On June 1, 1973, Robert pleaded guilty to manslaughter and was sentenced to fifteen years in prison. After his release Robert was murdered by Colombo crime family associates from Brooklyn on orders from Colombo crime family capo John Matera. Anthony Senter married an Italian-American woman on July 24, 1977 at a catering hall in Canarsie, Brooklyn. The wedding was attended by many criminals including Gambino crime family associate Roy DeMeo. Joseph Carmine Testa was born 1955 in the United States. Testa was one of nine children born to a transport truck driver and a housewife. His brother Patrick Testa also became a mobster joining the DeMeo crew. Growing up Anthony Senter became close friends with Joseph Testa. When Testa was fifteen, a thirteen year old neighbor was mugged by a knife wielding Puerto-Rican man from East New York. The assaulted victim complained to Testa, who gathered Senter among others, and led the group in a borrowed car spending the day searching for the assailant. In 1973, Testa was nearly killed in a bar fight with a Puerto-Rican opponent when the assailants knife punctured his lung. Senter hunted down the Puerto-Rican and nearly beat him to death with his fists. Testa was considered more dangerous by reputation than Senter among criminal associates. By 1970, Senter had already been convicted of auto theft three times by the age of 12. Testa and Senter were successful in having all of their cases dismissed because they were juveniles at the time. Testa and Senter became known as the Gemini twins because they were always together and the primary hangout of the DeMeo crew was the Gemini Lounge. Chris Rosenberg hired Senter and Testa to wax his Corvette and Porsche and steal cars for him. Rosenberg introduced his friends Senter and Testa to Roy DeMeo who asked them to join his crew. DeMeo, Rosenberg, Senter and Testa became the core of the DeMeo crew who became notorious for their ruthless violence. The crew was suspected to be involved in 75 to 200 murders throughout the mid- 1970s and into the early 1980s, when the majority of the crew members still alive were brought to justice. When Senter joined the DeMeo crew, he gained a reputation as a sadistic killer who enjoyed mutilating his victims. Senter also gained a reputation for providing the crew with significant revenue from auto theft. Senter and Testa were both full-blooded Italians and were eligible to be inducted into the mafia. Although, Senter was a large earner for the Gemini Lounge crew he was highly disliked by Albert DeMeo, the son of Roy DeMeo. Albert's personal judgment of Senter was that, "there was something slick and phony about him". He had a collapsed lung from a near fatal knife fight and chain smoked. He was always to be seen pressing his hand against his chest and complaining that he couldn't breathe. On January 10, 1983, Roy DeMeo went to crew member Patrick Testa's body shop for a meeting with his men. A few days later, on January 18, he was found murdered in his abandoned car's trunk. He had been shot multiple times in the head and had a bullet wound in his hand, assumed by law enforcement as being from throwing his hand up to his face in a self-defense reflex when the shots were fired at him. Anthony Gaggi was originally suspected by law enforcement officials of being the one who personally killed DeMeo. Gaggi was not charged with the crime. According to Anthony Casso, DeMeo was killed at Patrick Testa's Canarsie home by Joseph Testa and Senter following an agreement with Casso, who was given the contract by Gambino crime family Boss Paul Castellano and Frank DeCicco after they were unable to kill DeMeo in the fall of 1982. DeMeo was seated, about to receive coffee, when Testa and Senter opened fire. Anthony Gaggi was not present. After the murder of Roy DeMeo, Senter and Testa drifted into the Lucchese crime family. According to former Lucchese acting boss Anthony Casso, they were responsible for the murder on June 13, 1986 of Russian-American gangster Vladimir Reznikov. Reznikov had reportedly threatened the life and family of Marat Balagula, a Ukrainian immigrant who ruled the Russian Mafia in Brighton Beach. Balagula, who was then masterminding a

multi-million dollar gasoline bootlegging operation, had been paying tribute to the Five Families, who regarded him as their biggest moneymaker after drugs.
On September 14, 1989, Senter and Testa were both sentenced to life imprisonment. As of June 12, 2011, Senter continues to serve his sentence at the United States Penitentiary (USP), Allenwood, Pennsylvania. Testa is currently serving the sentence at Federal Correctional Complex, Butner for crimes that include multiple murders. In 1994, it was discovered that pension dues were being paid into a Teamsters pension account in Senter's name by a cousin of Senter, one Dominic Vulpis, who owned a garbage company. A court investigator determined that $30,000 of dues had been paid into the account over a six-year period all the while Senter was in prison on a life sentence. Union officials said Senter could have qualified for a pension of $1,400 a month if the payments by Canarsie Recycling had continued for another five years. Senter will not collect the pension - the Teamsters disqualified Senter as a member and barred his pension. It is unclear if Senter's cousin, Dominic Vulpis, or the garbage company he owns received a refund of the fraudulent dues.

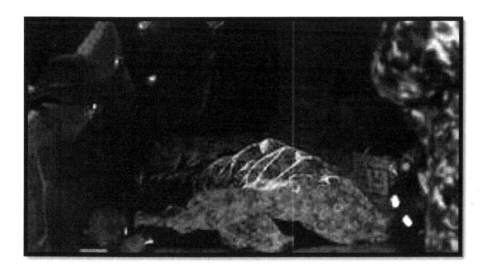

Mr. Casso. None.

Senator ROTH. Now, you testified about pleading guilty to a 72-count indictment, including murder, racketeering and extortion. How many murders?

[Pause.]

Mr. Casso. I believe 16.

Senator ROTH. I am sorry, I could not hear you.

Mr. Casso. I believe 16.

Alleged member of Russian Organized Crime

Senator ROTH. Was Joey Testa every charged with killing Reznikov, and where is he today?

Mr. Casso. He was never charged with that murder, and he is at a Federal prison also.

Senator ROTH. Now, you stated that you are a "made" member of the Lucchese family. Would you please explain what that means and describe the initiation ceremony by which you became a "made" member?

Mr. Casso. To become a "made" member, you have to be sponsored by a captain of the family, who would bring you to the boss of the family and sponsor you to become a "made" member. They have a ceremony with the boss, the Consiglieri, and the underbosses present at that time, and the captain who brings you in. They prick your trigger finger and make it bleed, and then they put it on a little piece of paper; they set it on fire, and you burn it in your hand, and you repeat after them that you will never betray La Cosa Nostra, or you will burn like the paper is burning in your hand. And your life does not belong to you anymore; your life belongs to them.

Alleged member of Russian Organized Crime

Senator ROTH. Now, we know that the Lucheses were not the only organized crime family involved with the Russians in the gas tax business. What role did you play in getting other La Cosa Nostra families involved in this gas tax scam?

Mr. Casso. Well, what we did was — the Colombo boss came to see me, and we put it together — the Russians wanted to put it together so there was no more problem, the Russians would get paid, and everyone would not steal each other's stops, and put everything above board. So the Genovese family had a branch in the gasoline business also, with their own group of Russians. What I did was I reached out for the Genovese family; I met with them, I met with their underboss. I told them we wanted to have a meeting with the Colombo family, the Lucchese family and the Genovese family, and that the people we have running the gasoline business for us who go up front and handle this every day with the Russians have a meeting, and let us all make this one; we will put it together, and everyone earns an equal share. And this is what we did.

We had this meeting. They agreed. We put it together. Being that everyone agreed, we turned around, and we told the Russians that they would have to pay a tax of a penny a gallon to us, to our three families, which totaled maybe $500,000 a month. And they agreed upon this; they were very happy because they could run their business without having a problem from anyone.

So now we had three families involved. We had the Genovese family, the Lucheses, and the Colombo family. And we ran like that until about 1988. In 1988, the Gambino family wanted to get involved. They also had a Russian group that they were working with, but in a little smaller way, and that group was interfering with what we put together.

So we took it upon ourselves — we had another meeting about the Gambino family and if we were going to invite them into the cartel that we put together, which we did; we made it a 4-way split. And we had four groups — the Gambinos had a Russian group, the Lucheses had their own Russian group, the Colombos had Markowitz and his Russian group, and the Genovese family had their own. We just combined it like that, and it was running smooth.

Senator ROTH. Do you know if these kinds of agreements are still in effect?

Mr. Casso. In the present, as far as I know, yes.

Senator ROTH. As far as you know, yes?

Mr. Casso. Yes.

Senator ROTH. Are you aware of any other murders committed by the La Cosa Nostra families on behalf of Russian organized crime in connection with gas tax schemes?

Mr. Casso. I know there were a couple of murders with Russians with the Gambino group, but I do not really know their names. But I know a couple of murders took place with them, with their group.

Senator ROTH. How would you characterize the Russians as business partners?

Mr. Casso. They are good businessmen. They are good businessmen, and as far as money-wise, whatever you have coming to you, they always made much more money than they gave organized crime, than we got. But we always knew that.

Senator ROTH. Senator Cohen?

Senator Cohen. Thank you, Mr. Chairman. Mr. Casso, how did you get the name "Gaspipe"?

Mr. Casso. They have been calling me that since a very early age, when I was a teenager. It was like a family name, and being that I was the youngest out of 3 children, it stuck with me.

Senator COHEN. No association with your activities, the nickname?

Mr. Casso. None whatsoever.

Surveillance photo FBI

Senator COHEN. You mentioned going to the hierarchy of authority when Senator ROTH asked you why Marat came to you as such. You said he was just simply proceeding on a one of authority, basically, that it was the proper thing to do. So you had your own organizational structure, since you were the enforcers, basically, or the protectors of Marat, I assume.

Alleged member of Russian Organized Crime

Mr. Casso. Yes, right.

Senator Cohen. OK. Do the Russian criminal gangs have the same sort of hierarchical structure as any one of the Italian families as such — the Gambinos, the Colombos, the Lucheses? Do they have capos, consiglieris, underbosses, boss — do they have anything like that?

Mr. Casso. Not really.

Senator COHEN. So they are not structured?

Mr. Casso. Not in this country.

Senator COHEN. Not in this country.

Mr. Casso. No. They have gangs, or their own crews, the Russians, and mostly they are violent among themselves. This is why we handled it. We would never want Marat to go and get someone else, hurt someone else. We would rather him come, because maybe there is no need to hurt someone else. Maybe this is a situation where you can talk to someone and resolve the problem. But the Russians are not that way; they are a little hot-headed, and they are a little violent sometimes.

Senator Cohen. You indicated in your statement that they are not afraid to use violence. Do you mean they are not afraid to use violence against one another?

Alleged member of Russian Organized Crime

Mr. Casso. Right.

Senator Cohen. But they would not use violence against the Lucchese family members?

Mr. Casso. No.

Senator COHEN. Why do you think they had to come to you to get protection — they do not have enough muscle as such of their own that they would simply say, "We don't need to pay you a penny a gallon for our protection"?

Mr. Casso. It is not only protection; it is putting it together because, like Marat, he owned a couple of hundred gas stations. So when we put the cartel together, now no one else was going to go into his stations to sell gas a little cheaper, just to sell the gas, and they start fighting amongst themselves again. So we held peace, and, you know, protection goes more than one way.

Senator Cohen. And you indicated, finally, that the Gambino family came in toward the tail-end of this arrangement because they had a Russian connection as well. If another family comes along with a Russian connection, will they keep expanding the business?

Alleged member of Russian Organized Crime

Mr. Casso. No. To be honest with you, we just barely let the Gambino family in.

Senator Cohen. OK. That is all I have, Mr. Chairman.

Senator ROTH. Thank you, Senator Cohen. That is all that we require of you, Mr. Casso. I would ask that all spectators remain seated until the witness leaves the hearing room, and I would now direct the Capitol Police and the Marshals to accompany Mr. Casso from the hearing room.

Our next witness is a Russian criminal currently incarcerated in the United States. Again because of security concerns, the witness will be testifying anonymously from behind a screen to protect his identity.

As I said before, it is my understanding that members of the media have already been advised as to those locations in the hearing room where cameras will and will not be permitted during the course of this testimony, in order to maintain security. Prior to the entrance of this witness, I direct that all cameras be turned to face either to the rear or to the window side of the hearing room. I would ask the Capitol Police whether all cameras have been redirected and whether the hearing room is secure so that the witness may be brought in. Please bring him in.

I would say to the witness that we swear all witnesses who appear before the Subcommittee. I would ask that you remain seated while I administer the oath. Please raise your right hand. Do you swear or affirm that the testimony you will give before this Subcommittee is the truth, the whole truth, and nothing but the truth, so help you, God?

Anonymous Russian Criminal. Yes, I do.

Senator ROTH. Please proceed with your testimony, and pull the microphone closer and speak up a little louder.

Alleged member of Russian Organized Crime

TESTIMONY OF AN ANONYMOUS RUSSIAN CRIMINAL

Anonymous Russian Criminal. Chairman ROTH, Members of the Subcommittee, good afternoon. I have been asked to testify today about Russian organized crime in the United States, a problem which exists in several cities and is likely to grow.

Let me explain the two reasons why I am able to speak on this subject. First,' I grew up in Russia with people who are now leaders of criminal groups worldwide, including here in the United States.

My father was a high-ranking officer in the Soviet military, and so as a boy, I attended the best schools and socialized with the Community Party elite. My classmates included many future politicians and criminal leaders.

Second, since 1992, I have lived in the United States and know many of the Russian criminals who have settled here. Some of these men, such as Leonid Zuza and Vyacheslav Kirillovich Ivankov, or "Taponchik," might be familiar to you. They are to me.

Alleged member of Russian Organized Crime

What you have to understand is that the well-to-do Russian community in this country is rather small and that the successful Russian criminals are part of it. Through my business and social contacts, I was a part of this community, but I have been in prison for the past year. I am serving a sentence for the possession of a firearm, which violated the terms of my probation agreement. I am testifying behind this screen today because I believe that if my identity were known, I or my family might be killed.

To understand Russian organized crime in this country, you must first appreciate the situation in Russia. For the 2 years prior to my arrival in the United States, I set up and ran the Moscow branch of an American corporation specializing in investments and international trade. We had a beautiful office 3 minutes from Red Square.

Now, there are two things you must do to operate a business successfully in Moscow. First, you must pay the right government officials under the table. Because I had known officials in Moscow since I was a child, figuring out whom to pay was simple. To set up our office so close to Red Square, I had to pay money to the chief of government property in Moscow. Later, when we wanted to open a supermarket in Moscow, I paid cash to the mayor of Moscow, Yuri Luzhkov.

Alleged member of Russian Organized Crime

The second thing you must do to run a successful business is purchase a "krisha," literally, "roof," in Russian, which has come to mean protection. The more important you are, the higher the roof must be. In Moscow, organized crime provides the roof.

Back in 1990, I could pay one organized crime group, say, 10 to 20 percent of our profits, and it would make sure that I did not have trouble with any other groups. There was crime, but at least it was orderly. Leaders of the major organized crime groups in Moscow would meet regularly to divide up opportunities. But as time went on, things got out of control. Fighting broke out among the organized crime groups in Moscow, and several of the leaders were assassinated. Otari Kvantrishvili, at that time the most powerful organized crime figure in Moscow and a friend of mine, was the first to be killed. Several others followed. Most of these men were "vory v zakone," a title reserved for powerful Russian godfathers. As I said, things got out of control. I did not know which roofs to pay and which were safe to ignore. Men were showing up regularly and demanding protection money. I came to the United States to escape this turmoil, and I can tell you that many criminals have as well. Some are thugs who worked as enforcers or muscle in groups based in Russia. These men are responsible for much of the violence that has taken place in Brighton Beach and other communities where Russians are concentrated in this country.

Alleged member of Russian Organized Crime

These men are also disorganized and looking for a leader to devise a profitable criminal venture; someone like Ivankov. These are dangerous men, but would be far more so behind a clever leader.

There is a difference between the Russian criminal who immigrates to the United States today and the one who came in the 1970's and 1980's. Fifteen years ago, Russian immigrant criminals were on the whole smarter than today's lot. The schemes they executed — Balagula's fuel tax evasion, the medical insurance fraud of the Smushkevich Brothers — made them millionaires. As I said before, most of the current wave of Russians is more prone to violence, but less resourceful than their predecessors. Whether or not they left Russia with money, they will run out, and they will be looking for ways to make more.

Alleged member of Russian Organized Crime

Russian organized crime in this country includes criminals from both immigrant waves. They are involved in a number of illegal activities, many of which I understand you have heard about earlier today. These range from money laundering to extortion to car theft to drug smuggling to insurance and gas tax fraud to murder. Some of these crimes, I know about specifically.

For example, I know of Russian criminals in this country who ship guns and cocaine back to Russia. These men have beautiful offices in Rockefeller Center and Beverly Hills and look like legitimate businessmen. They run import-export businesses funded by the mafia over in Moscow. Much of what they trade in is legal, but much is also illegal.

For instance, they purchase cocaine in the United States for $20 to $30 a gram and sell it in Moscow for $100 to $150. In Moscow, cocaine is a habit of the very rich, which means only three types of people can afford it — newly-rich businessmen and politicians, prostitutes, and criminals.

Alleged member of Russian Organized Crime

I know of murders as well. I knew Oleg Koratayev, the famous Russian boxer who was shot and killed in Brighton Beach outside the Arbat Restaurant. I know also that in the summer of 1994, Leonid Zuza ordered the murder of another ex-boxer named "Dmitry" because he refused to pay Zuza $17,000 he owed him. The killer, a Russian named "Vladimir" who worked for Zuza shot Dmitry on a patio outside a cafe on Melrose Avenue in Los Angeles.

I also know about extortion, which Russian criminals practice all over the world, mainly on fellow Russians. I myself was approached by a group of Russian criminals. They showed me pictures of my family. They did not have to tell me why. What they meant was that if I did not pay them money, my family would be harmed or killed. They demanded tens of thousands of dollars. The leader of the group came to my house one night to collect this money from me, but I had a shotgun in my house, and he chose to leave.

Alleged member of Russian Organized Crime

Professional hockey players from the former Soviet Union are also victims of extortion. And the extortion does not just happen in Moscow or Kiev; it happens here. Alexander Mogilny, who plays for the Vancouver Canucks, was threatened by Sergei Fomitchev, a man I know. Fomitchev had helped Mogilny come to this country.

A couple of years ago, Fomitchev came to Mogilny, threatened him and demanded money. Mogilny was scared and went to the police, who caught Fomitchev before anything happened. Fomitchev has ties to Russian organized crime groups.

Boss Semion Mogilevich

Often, when a Russian criminal demands money, the threat is not explicit, but it is clearly understood. Alexei Zhitnick, a defenseman for the Buffalo Sabres, used to play for the Los Angeles Kings. He showed up at a Russian club in Los Angeles one night with a new car, expensive clothes and beautiful women. He was young and naive. A man named Sasha, whom I know is connected with a Russian criminal group, approached Alexei and demanded money from him. Sasha was sending Alexei a warning, to make sure he thought about his future in Los Angeles. Alexei did not go to the police. Instead, he went to a more powerful criminal group to take care of the problem for him, which I understand it did.

I also know Vladimir Malakhov, who plays for the Montreal Canadians, but used to be with the New York Islanders. He was approached in the National Restaurant in Brighton Beach by a man who worked for Ivankov. The man demanded money from Malakhov. He did not have to threaten him explicitly; the message was clearly understood. Malakhov spent the next months in fear, looking over his shoulder to see if he was being followed, avoiding restaurants and clubs where Russian criminals hang out. Fortunately, the problem went away when Malakhov was traded to Montreal.

These are just a few stories to illustrate the illegal activities of Russian organized crime in the United States. What we have here cannot compare to the criminal activity and structure in Russia. But what we have here is a problem that is growing. Just last week, I heard that another "vory v zakone," or Russian godfather, recently arrived in the United States. As I said, when leaders arrive, the problems will multiply. I am happy to answer your questions.

Alleged member of Russian Organized Crime

Senator ROTH. You stated that there are companies in the United States exporting weapons and drugs to the former Soviet Union. What kind of weapons are being shipped, and who is buying them?

Anonymous Russian Criminal. The most recent from the United States to Russian are shotguns and handguns, a lot of equipment like bulletproof vests and walkie-talkie radios.

Senator ROTH. And who is buying them?

Anonymous Russian Criminal. These weapons are bought by criminal groups and new businessmen.

Senator ROTH. Now, you testified about the money paid to government officials before you could open a business in Moscow. Would an American businessman who wanted to set up an office in Moscow also have to bribe the appropriate official?

Alleged member of Russian Organized Crime

Anonymous Russian Criminal. Yes; usually, it is more through his business connections and his business partners.

Senator ROTH. You testified about the extortion in this country of hockey players from the former Soviet Union. There have been reports that players or their families have also been threatened when they return home to the former Soviet Union during the offseason. Is that correct?

Anonymous Russian Criminal. Yes, sir.

Senator ROTH. And in the case of the professional hockey player, Alexei Zhitnick, why didn't he go to the police after he was threatened?

Alexei Zhitnick

Anonymous Russian Criminal. Because he does not trust police; nobody trusts police in Russia. He would just go to a powerful criminal group to protect him.

Alleged member of Russian Organized Crime

Senator ROTH. No trust in the police because of his past?

Anonymous Russian Criminal. Yes.

Senator ROTH. You testified that many of the criminals who have arrived not long ago in the United States are more violent than the older generation of criminals from the former Soviet Union. What has caused this change?

Alleged member of Russian Organized Crime

Anonymous Russian Criminal. Because the new criminals who are arriving in the United States are less educated, more violent and disorganized, and they are ready for any job to make money.

Senator ROTH. You also stated that you heard of a Russian godfather who recently arrived in the United States. Who is the person you are referring to?

Anonymous Russian Criminal. His name is Vladimir, nicknamed "Rezni"; he is a godfather and friend of Ivankov.

Senator ROTH. We have heard testimony that Ivankov is one of the most powerful Russian organized crime figures to come to the United States. Why did he come to this country?

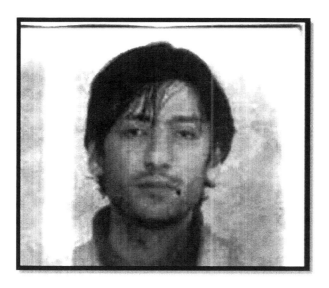

Alleged member of Russian Organized Crime

Anonymous Russian Criminal. To my understanding, I think there are two reasons. The first is to try to escape from Russian law enforcement, and the second is because he does not want to be killed, like a lot of his friends.

Senator ROTH. In your testimony, you observe that fighting among organized crime groups in Russia is causing criminals to come to the United States. What is causing this turmoil?

Anonymous Russian Criminal. They are fighting for power and for territory.

Senator ROTH. Power and territory?

Anonymous Russian Criminal. Yes, sir.

Alleged member of Russian Organized Crime

Senator ROTH. Do Russian criminals located in different U.S. cities communicate with each other, and is there communication between criminals in Russia and those in the United States?

Anonymous Russian Criminal. Yes. Several groups in New York and Seattle will fly and meet each other to look for business opportunities. I know that Ivankov flew several times from New York to Los Angeles and back.

Senator ROTH. How are Russian criminals able to get into the United States?

Anonymous Russian Criminal. It is very simple. They probably can buy phony passports for $200 or $300 and get visas at the U.S. Embassy, probably, in the commercial section of the U.S. Embassy, and come to the United States.

Senator ROTH. Those are all the questions I have. Prior to your exit, again I want to direct that all cameras be turned to face either to the rear or the window side of the hearing room. I will ask the Capitol Police whether all cameras have been redirected. I will now ask the Capitol Police and the Marshals to accompany the witness from thc hearing room.

Alleged member of Russian Organized Crime

Senator ROTH. Our final witnesses are a panel of local law enforcement officers who specialize in investigating Russian organized crime cases in the United States. One of these witnesses is an undercover officer who will be testifying anonymously from behind a screen and with the benefit of voice distortion to protect his identity. Again, it is my understanding that members have been advised as to the locations in the hearing room where cameras will and will not be permitted during the course of this testimony in order to maintain security. So at this time, I direct that all cameras be turned to face either to the rear or to the window side of the hearing room and ask the Capitol Police whether all cameras have been so directed.

The hearing room is secure, and the witness may be brought in. The other witnesses on this panel are Detective Dan Mackey and Ralph Cefarello of the New York City Police Department, and Detective William Pollard of the Los Angeles Police Department.

Gentlemen, it is a pleasure to welcome you. As you know, we swear in all witnesses. Again, I would ask the witness behind the screen not to stand for the swearing in; the others, I would ask to please stand and raise your right hand. Do you swear or affirm that the testimony you will give to the Subcommittee today is the truth, the whole truth, and nothing but the truth, so help you, God?

Mr. Cefarello. I do.

Mr. Mackey. I do.

Mr. Pollard. I do.

Anonymous Witness. I do.

Senator ROTH. Thank you, gentlemen. Please be seated We will begin our testimony with Detective Mackey. Again, I will ask you to summarize; your full statement, of course, will be included in the record as if read.

TESTIMONY OF DANIEL MACKEY AND RALPH CEFARELLO. DETECTIVES, NEW YORK CITY POLICE DEPARTMENT

Mr. Mackey. Good afternoon. Chairman ROTH, Senator Lieberman and Members of the Permanent Subcommittee on Investigations. My name is Detective Daniel Mackey of the New York City Police Department. On behalf of myself and my colleague, Detective Ralph Cefarello, thank you for this opportunity to testify about Russian/Eurasian criminals operating in New York City and what is being done to stop them.

Previous speakers have given you international and national perspectives. Our view of this most serious crime problem is that of working detectives, catching cases involving suspects and quite often victims who were born in the former Soviet Union.

I work in a precinct detective squad that covers Brighton Beach, Brooklyn. Since the late 1970's, Brighton Beach has become home to an ever-growing number of Russian-speaking immigrants from a variety of former Soviet republics, including Georgia, Azerbaijan and Chechnya. The great majority are hardworking, law-abiding citizens who have revitalized a neighborhood that has come to be known as "Little Odessa." Brighton Beach Avenue is lined with thriving markets, restaurants, nightclubs, clothing and video stores that all cater to Russian-speaking customers. It is possible to go about your daily business in Brighton Beach without uttering or reading one word of English.

Unfortunately, Brighton Beach is also a hub for Russian-born criminals with a well-deserved reputation for extreme violence. Their criminal activities include vicious murders and assaults, extortion of Russian-owned businesses, prostitution, illegal gambling, and a vast collection of frauds and schemes that ravage the economy, causing government, businesses and consumers millions of dollars.

We have encountered staged motor vehicle accidents in which all participants claim back and neck injuries, then file insurance claims for medical services provided by Russian-operated medical groups also believed to be in on the scam. Additionally, we have, in joint operations with the United States Secret Service, dismantled sizeable cellular phone-cloning networks run by Russian/Eurasian nationals.

While we have had some success, it is often difficult, and frankly, quite frustrating to investigate these illegal activities — for the same reasons it has always been difficult and frustrating to investigate crimes committed within a close-knit immigrant community. To a large extent, the criminals count on language as a barrier as well as a presumed reluctance on the part of fellow immigrants to cooperate with the police, especially if the police in their homeland were viewed as agents of an oppressive regime.

The NYPD has relatively few police officers and investigators who are fluent in Russian. The language barrier may hinder an investigation in several ways. The first officers or detectives to arrive at a crime scene may have to scramble for translators. And it is tougher to field traditional undercover operations used in public morals cases.

For example, Russian-run brothels are extremely lucrative but do not cater to non-Russian clients. We have attempted to use undercover "Johns" who do speak Russian, but even they require an introduction from a credible go-between, which has proven difficult to obtain.

We have investigated numerous cases involving the extortion of Russian-owned businesses, sometimes referred to as "window insurance" or "protection money." It is not uncommon for complainants in these cases to cooperate only up until the time an arrest is made, then refuse to follow through on the prosecution. When the crime is murder, witnesses willing to cooperate are also scarce. At this time, I would like to introduce Detective Cefarello, who will provide a brief overview of our experience with murder investigations of Russian crime figures.

Senator ROTH. Detective Cefarello?

Mr. Cefarello. Good afternoon. My name is Detective Ralph Cefarello. I am currently assigned to a new citywide investigative unit specifically created to combat the criminal activity you are hearing about today.

In the past 15 years, there has been a total of 42 murders and 24 attempted murders in New York City known to be linked to Russian/Eurasian criminal organizations. Many of the murder victims served time in prison in the former Soviet Union or were known to engage in criminal activity there. Several were accomplished athletes in contact sports such as wrestling, boxing, or one of the martial arts. Commonly, the motive for these murders involved disputes over profits from illegal activities and turf battles over extortion rights. Witnesses in these cases were often less than forthcoming. Take, for example, the murder in Brooklyn of a former Soviet heavyweight champion. This individual, who was involved in strong-arm extortion and narcotics trafficking, was shot and killed in front of a Russian nightclub on Brighton Beach Avenue. He had been among some 75 guests at a private party. His killer had also been present during the festivities. We talked to everyone who had been present at the party. The story was the same, interview after interview: No one saw or heard anything. No one could identify the victim. No one could identify his killer. Despite these types of investigative obstacles, we have been able to clear 15 of these 42 homicides, and we expect to prosecute those responsible for numerous other murders pursuant to active RICO investigations with Federal prosecutors.

It is important to note that cooperation among local, State and Federal law enforcement agencies remains an essential ingredient of any successful strategy to address this problem. NYPD detectives meet regularly with representatives of other agencies. These information-sharing sessions have proven quite productive. Finally, thank you for your interest in a crime problem we are working so hard to eradicate. We already enjoy the leadership and support of Mayor Rudolph W. Giuliani and Police Commissioner Howard Safir. Any additional Federal resources you could send our way would be greatly appreciated and well-used to permanently stunt the growth of Russian organized crime criminal activity on our shores.

Senator ROTH. Thank you, Mr. Cefarello. Mr. Pollard?

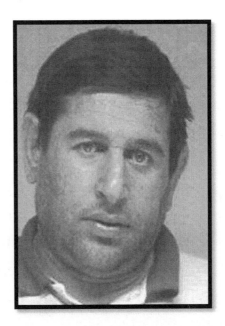

Alleged member of Russian Organized Crime

TESTIMONY OF WILLIAM POLLARD, DETECTIVE, ORGANIZED CRIME INTELLIGENCE DIVISION, LOS ANGELES POLICE DEPARTMENT

Mr. Pollard. Good afternoon, Senator ROTH, Members of the Subcommittee. I am Detective William Pollard, Los Angeles Police Department, Organized Crime Intelligence Division.

I will present abbreviated remarks regarding organized crime in the Los Angeles area, and I request that my full written statement be entered into the record.

"Russian organized crime" is a term covering more than 150 ethnic backgrounds and 120 languages. The common denominator is the Russian language, spoken by most due to the Soviet rule for 70 years or so.

Historically, in the greater Los Angeles area, the problem started in the mid-seventies when the Soviets released Russian Jews and Armenians, and they came to the United States as refugees. In these groups of émigrés were criminal elements that, upon arriving here, continued their criminal activities. In fact, some of the émigrés who were admitted as Jewish refugees were not even Jewish and had spent time in Russian prison. At the same time, Armenian refugees were also arriving in the United States with a similar pattern, having a percentage of criminals.

It is also believed that the Soviet Union used the refugee program to send KGB agents and operatives into our population. Since the breakup of the Soviet Union, we see a much more diverse ethnic background in the criminal element coming here. Currently, the greater Los Angeles area has the second-largest Russian-speaking population, excluding Armenians, in the United States and the largest population of Armenians outside of Armenia.

The city of Glendale, which adjoins the city of Los Angeles, finds that 25 percent of their population is Armenian, with half of those being Soviet or Russian Armenian.

Along with our resident populations, there is a growing number of tourist or "shadow people," transient individuals who come and go, many times engaging in criminal activities. While in the past, no real structure was observed in the Jewish or Armenian groups, today, investigators from the Los Angeles Police Department and the Glendale Police Department see a growth of structures in several Armenian criminal groups.

Other Russian groups that still do not appear to have a structure in the United States seem to be arms of structured groups in the former Soviet Union. This lack of observable structure is the main reason why law enforcement in Southern California did not see organized crime as the upcoming problem it is today. Over the years, what were first seen as career-type criminals committing extortions on their own and frauds against our society, with a small amount of violence, now commit very sophisticated, major frauds and a high degree of violence. Much of this is due to the background of the new criminal who may have been a KGB agent, a police officer, a politician, or a well-educated professional in his country.

A few years ago, the Glendale Police Department arrested a former police chief of the city of Yerevan, Armenia's capitol, on charges of extortion, rape, and kidnapping.

Some examples of the types of criminal activities that have been investigated by law enforcement in the greater Los Angeles area are the following. In 1983, a Russian businessman became indebted to organized crime figures for $50,000 at a 30 percent interest rate.

For the next 8 years, he had to borrow another $70,000 to make payments. During that time, he repaid $480,000. In 1991, he and his family were being threatened by organized crime figure for repayment, and he finally came to law enforcement for help. The suspects were arrested, and we had two convictions in that case.

Nineteen ninety-one was also the year that the Smushkevich Brothers were arrested on the basis of a task force investigation involving Federal, State and local agencies. The medical fraud included false billing through mobile medical laboratories and doctors' offices. This was the largest medical care fraud case in U.S. history. Fraudulent billings were in excess of $1 billion.

In 1992, a few Russian visitors to Los Angeles who had been made indentured servants in a scheme to commit fraud with checks and credit cards wished to return home to Russia. The Russians running the scheme would not allow the visitors to leave and held their passports and visas. An argument ensued, and the visitors murdered the two Russian captors. Los Angeles County sheriffs responded to a call from the neighbors regarding a car in the driveway with the motor running for a long period of time and discovered the suspects attempting to eliminate identification on the bodies by removing the fingertips and removing the bullets from the bodies.

In 1994, a group of Armenians who had been extorting, kidnapping and in general terrorizing the Armenian community for the past 13 years were arrested and convicted.

In 1995, a task force of the Los Angeles Office FBI, IRS, Department of Defense, California Department of Justice, the Los Angeles Police Department and the Long Beach Police Department investigating fuel tax fraud that also involved using fraudulent IRS forms, rigging fuel pumps and blending additives to extend fuel concluded by arresting 25 individuals on various RICO violations. The ringleader, Joe Mikhailian, was identified as the "godfather" of the Armenian mafia in Los Angeles.

Current joint investigations are underway with the Los Angeles Police Department, the Glendale Police Department, and the FBI on a number of murders involving the garment industry. There have been 5 murders, 5 attempted murders, shootings, bombings and extortions in the Los Angeles-Glendale communities that are believed to be related to organized crime in the garment industry.

Of all of these crimes, there has only been one conviction for murder.

There are numerous investigations by several agencies into ongoing medical frauds, many of which have spread into other States as pressure is applied in the Southern California area. These frauds seem to be based on staged or manufactured auto accidents and involve not only doctors, but attorneys as well. Law enforcement is trying to combat the rapidly growing problem of Russian organized crime by working together on cases and forming task forces needed to solve the problem. In 1991, the Los Angeles Police Department, the Los Angeles FBI, and the Los Angeles County Sheriff's Office organized a regional meeting of law enforcement professionals known as the Soviet Organized Crime Intelligence Team, or "SOCIT." The California Department of Justice has been taking information from all sources and building a database on Russian organized crime to benefit law enforcement in tracking the problem. It also has been instrumental in organizing two more information-sharing groups in Northern California.

Some of the problems for law enforcement in dealing with the new criminals include a lack of trust in the community of law enforcement based on their experiences in the old country. Immigrants are subjected to threats from mafia members and feel that they have nowhere to turn. Law enforcement must make inroads into the community to build trust. They must also interact with other agencies on the local. State, national and international levels to counteract the highly mobile, violent Russian criminals who today deal with any other crime group in the world to continue their criminal enterprise.

Prosecutors need to be educated on the subject and make every effort to prosecute every case, no matter how trivial it may seem. There also needs to be an international database open to all law enforcement. Today, with the rapid growth of this problem, it is imperative that agencies and departments find resources for training, manpower and equipment to effectively combat the problem.

This concludes my statement. I will be happy to answer questions.

Senator ROTH. Thank you, Mr. Pollard. We will now hear from the undercover police officer. Please proceed.

Alleged member of Russian Organized Crime

TESTIMONY OF AN ANONYMOUS UNDERCOVER POLICEOFFICER FROM ANOTHER CITY

Anonymous Witness. Senators, I welcome the opportunity to appear before your distinguished committee.

I was born and raised in Russia. I emigrated from Russia to the United States in the 1970's. I have been a law enforcement officer for more than 15 years. I have served in different capacities — uniformed patrol, homicide detective and narcotics detective.

During the past 2 years, I have been involved in numerous Russian organized crime investigations.

Due to the fact that I am involved in a number of extremely sensitive investigations, I am testifying anonymously in order not to jeopardize these cases or the safety of others.

As I said earlier, I grew up on the former Soviet Union. I was raised under the Communist system, and I believe that I know the thinking of the people who were brought up in that system.

I am very active in the Russian émigré community in the city in which I live. I attend most of the gatherings of the émigrés and continue to be very much in touch with the Russian émigrés and their culture. I receive and read most of the literature that is published in the Russian language in both the former Soviet Union as well as here in the United States.

Now I would like to touch on the subject of the difference between the cultures in the Republics of the former Soviet Union and the United States.

During the Communist regime, for many people in the former USSR, the moral values accepted in a free society were "destroyed," maybe with a few exceptions. Russian people grew up with the understanding that stealing something from their place of employment is not a crime — maybe because one was not stealing from a friend but rather from a system.

They also grew up with the understanding that the rules were made to be bent or bypassed. That mentality, philosophy and upbringing explains why some of the Russian émigrés, many of whom were educated, family people, got involved in white collar-type criminal activity here in the United States.

Up until perestroika, the method by which success was judged in the USSR was the level of a person's education. Doctors, engineers, teachers and scientists were all accorded a somewhat higher status in society. Wealth was not a factor as a worker in a factory was making as much money as a doctor did. And the people who did make money in the underground economy or black market operations were concealing their wealth.

After perestroika, this situation was reversed, and the wealthy people rose to the top of society. With perestroika, organized crime flourished in Russia.

Now I would like to explain how these criminal groups emerged.

There were a number of young people who were energetic but impatient or unable to build up their own businesses over a period of time. These people started to form criminal groups based on their affiliations with neighborhoods, cities, or ethnicity. The groups were led by either professional criminals or people with leadership abilities and similar interests. These groups started to prey on the new Russian business society. They continued to grow, and some of the criminal organizations are now several thousand members strong. They would extort money, kidnap people for ransom, and organized collection agencies which used very unorthodox methods.

Another new industry began to emerge, that of "murder for hire." Business people would use these hired killers to wipe out their competition and thereby give a lesson to others: Do not fool around with my company or the area that I am operating in.

Information has been developed that many of these murders were committed in Russia by people with extensive military backgrounds. These actions forced the business people to each begin

looking for "protection." And a new and very profitable business, called "krisha," meaning "roof in English, came into being. Very few businesses in Russia could survive without this protection. Up to 50 percent of their income was diverted by the legitimate businesses to criminal organizations in return for this
 protection.

With the new ability to travel freely, we see Russian criminal organizations establishing their roots, their ties, here in the United States of America.

Another important point is that during the Communist regime, there was in effect a system where a privileged class of the Communist government officials was developed. There was almost a closed society of the Communist bureaucracy, and it was nearly impossible to become a part of it unless one was well-connected. However, with the dismantling of the Soviet Union, these people remained in office, but no longer under the Communist system which guaranteed them a better life. They began to see that money is the criterion on which people were judged; yet they had the power to issue licenses, permits, valuable government contracts, set customs duties on goods imported into the former Soviet Union, or set standards for the export of Russia's valuable commodities — for example, its natural resources.

Many of these government officials began to take advantage of their positions due to this perception. They or members of their families became "partners" in business enterprises or in effect "sold" their power and authority.

Information developed shows that many Russian government officials, working on a modest salary, amassed vast sums in this fashion. These same corrupt officials put the profits from this activity in bank accounts all over the world and purchase real estate or other property in various countries, including the United States of America.

In addition, many of the former intelligence and law enforcement agents and leaders perceived that they were "on the bottom," so to speak, of the new and emerging wealthy Russian society. Their services and knowledge became a valuable commodity to the emerging criminal groups.

In speaking with a number of sources of information over the past couple of years, I have learned that individuals and businesses affiliated with the former Soviet intelligence organizations are being used by the Russian organized crime groups all over the world, including in the United States. While I cannot go into the specifics of this, I can say that the information developed shows that the former intelligence officers are working in league with Russian organized crime and making huge profits in the process.

Among the strongest Russian criminal organizations which are operating today are the following groups. The Izmailovskaya organization, the Solntsevskaya organization, the Podolskaya organization, Balashikhin, Baumanskaya, Chechen criminal organizations, Dagestani, and the list goes on. This is just to name a few. We have been able to link several murders which have occurred in the United States to Russian organized crime groups. Information developed shows us that Russian criminals were open to co- operation with other criminal groups, for instance, Italian American criminal groups.

We also developed information about increasing cooperation be- tween Russian organized crime and Colombian drug cartels. The Russian organized crime groups are believed to be heavily involved in the laundering of the profits of these Colombian drug cartels. They have also established a continuous flow of cocaine from Colombia to Eastern Europe and Russia. It has even been recently re- ported in newspapers that drug dealers in Colombia are using former Soviet military transport aircraft to move quantities of cocaine.

To describe a typical activity of Russian organized crime in the United States, I can bring the following example. A hardworking Russian businessman operating in a heavily-populated Russian area of a major city is visited by several males. They tell the businessman that, either for a certain percentage of his business or regular payments, they will "protect" his business. If the business- man replies that he does not feel that he needs that protection, in the near future, strange things will happen to his family or him- self. Robberies may take place at his establishment. Acts of vandal- ism will occur. Threatening phone calls will be received, and/or violent acts against him or members of his family will take place.

Mikhail "French" Dyuzhev, alleged member of Russian organized crime

The same people will visit the businessman again and, now convinced that he does need protection, the businessman will start paying.

Senators I have been asked by your staff whether I have any advice for the Subcommittee on how to combat Russian organized crime. I would like to make a few suggestions that would come not only from me, but from law enforcement personnel with whom I am working on Federal, State and local levels.

Formal task forces should be established in major metropolitan areas, consisting of Federal, State and local officers. What these task forces could do is actively gather information about Russian organized crime activity in their cities and conduct investigations against these subjects. The task forces should establish liaison contacts with law enforcement agencies throughout the world, since Russian organized crime groups operate on a global level.

Alleged member of Russian organized crime Dmitri Morozov

One of the most glaring gaps in the fight against Russian organized crime is the lack of an extradition treaty between the United States of America and the former Soviet Republics. This has en- abled many Russian criminals associated with organized crime and sought as fugitives by Russian authorities to seek refuge in the

United States. By the same token, Russian criminals who have been committing crimes in the United States have subsequently left for Russia and found safe haven there.

What could be accomplished by addressing these matters, however, is a slowing down but not a complete halt to the growing problem of Russian organized crime in the United States of America. I thank you again for the opportunity to appear before your distinguished Subcommittee.

Senator ROTH. Detective Mackey, you stated that Brighton Beach is a hub for Russian-born criminals. Why is this true?

Alleged member of Russian Organized Crime

Mr. Mackey. That is correct. Chairman ROTH. Brighton Beach has traditionally been the first stop for new former Soviet Union émigrés, like the Chinatowns or Little Italy's or the like in New
York or other big cities. It is a small, oceanfront, tightly-knit community where networking, connections and ethnic alliance make Brighton Beach the ideal place to ply their trade.

The prevailing attitude of not wanting to be labeled a "stukatch," or informant, an attitude which is a residue of life in the former Soviet Union, makes Brighton Beach convenient for criminals. An example of this is indicated by pen registers or wire- taps of investigations outside of New York jurisdiction which lead back to Brighton Beach. No matter what agency or its jurisdiction, the tentacles of Brighton Beach are present.

Alleged member of Russian Organized Crime

Senator ROTH. Has Brighton Beach changed notably since the breakup of the Soviet Union and the resulting influx of Russian immigrants?

Mr. Mackey. Yes, Mr. Chairman. Changes in Brighton Beach that we have been observing include younger criminals in Brighton Beach with a propensity toward intimidation, with intelligence indicating that they have been sent here to specifically engage in criminal activity. Additionally, we have seen more violent acts than in the past, as indicated by a recent double homicide in which both victims were totally dismembered. Intelligence indicates that many of these criminals are transient, with the ability to move about freely.

Senator ROTH. You indicated that they were sent here; do you mean they may continue to have ties with criminal elements back in Russia?

Mr. Mackey. That is correct. Chairman ROTH. We have had intelligence briefings that indicate that these criminals plying their trade in Brighton Beach still travel back and forth freely between Brooklyn and the former Soviet Union.

Alleged member of Russian Organized Crime

Senator ROTH. Detective Cefarello, Anthony Casso testified earlier today about the killing of Vladimir Resnikov outside of the Odessa Restaurant in Brighton Beach. Are you familiar with this murder, and if so, has anybody been charged with this crime?

Mr. Cefarello. Yes, Chairman ROTH, I am familiar with the murder, and as of this time, no one has been charged in that murder.

Senator ROTH. Mr. Casso also testified that Resnikov was killed by Joey Testa of the Lucchese organized crime family. Is this a plausible explanation of the murder?

Mr. Cefarello. Yes, it is plausible. The murder investigation show witness statements and forensic and some individual statements that make that plausible, yes.

Senator ROTH. You testified that there have been more than 40 murders

Alleged member of Russian Organized Crime

Mr. Cefarello. Forty-two, yes.

Senator ROTH Forty-two — in New York City linked to Russian organized crime. What is the explanation as to why there have been so many murders? Have you found any recurring patterns or methods used by the Russians to commit these murders?

Mr. Cefarello. The prevalent weapon of choice used by Russians is usually a semiautomatic handgun, the high-powered semi-automatic handguns, although "street sweeper" shotguns and automatic machine pistols have been used. Several victims have been brutally stabbed, as Detective Mackey stated, and two were totally dismembered. As far as why they occur, I would say that probably as in any other organized crime organization in the past, it would probably have a lot to do with greed and someone trying to take over your territory or someone trying to get some of that tax money that you heard about earlier from the gas scams. With millions and millions of dollars passing hands, someone is going to get killed in between.

Alleged member of Russian Organized Crime

Senator ROTH. Do you think this is still continuing?

Mr. Cefarello. From what I have heard today and from what I have heard before, yes.

Senator ROTH. Detective Pollard, it is hard to see you because of the screen. You testified about "shadow people" who are hired by Russian organized criminal groups to travel to the United States to commit murder and other violent crimes. Can you provide us with examples of crimes in the Los Angeles area that you suspect were committed by these "shadow people"?

Mr. Pollard. Yes, Senator. Probably the best example would be the Carole Little murders, which is the garment industry case that I referred to. In that case, there have been 5 murders, 5 attempted murders, and numerous other violent crimes. It is well-believed that most of these, or a good percentage of them at least, have been done by these "shadow people" or visitors coming in.
It leaves detectives with dead-ends when they are investigating.

Senator ROTH. Did they go back to Russia afterwards — is that what happens?

Mr. Pollard. Yes. The information we get from the street sources indicates that they will come in on a flight from Moscow to Los Angeles on a Saturday; there is another flight from Los Angeles to Moscow on Wednesday. They will come in on one of those flights, do whatever they have been hired to do, and be out on the next flight.

Senator ROTH. In your statement. Detective Pollard, you discuss the problems of L-1 visa fraud enabling Russian criminals to enter the United States. How serious a problem is this, and what is being done, if anything, to help solve it?

Mr. Pollard. That problem is a serious problem right now. There is an ongoing investigation by the State Department that we are assisting with. The scenario on it is that a Russian crime figure will go to the Moscow Embassy and obtain a B-1 or B-2 visitor visa, will come to the United States, set up a storefront or a mail-drop-type business, write himself a letter of invitation, saying that he is needed for some work in that business, return to Moscow with the letter, take it back to the Embassy, trade in his visitor visa for a work visa and come back; he will then write more letters to more people in his organization in Russia and have them come here. They will use that storefront business to launder money and to cover whatever their criminal enterprise is.

Like I said, the State Department has an ongoing investigation nationwide on that; local and State agencies are assisting with feeding information and helping as they can.

Senator ROTH. I was struck by a line in your statement where a Russian source said, "The only thing I fear is deportation, and you won't do it." The Subcommittee has investigated the problem of criminal aliens, and the Senate recently adopted an amendment that I cosponsored to simplify and expedite the deportation of criminal agents. Do you believe that deportation is an effective weapon?

Mr. Pollard. Yes, sir. I think it would be a highly effective weapon if we could use it. The problems that have come up in the past as far as using it, especially with the refugee statuses, have been a real hindrance. With the changes that have been made and should be made in the future, I think it would be a very effective weapon.

Senator ROTH. I would now like to turn to our undercover officer. You discussed several organized crime groups based in the former Soviet Union. Do any of these groups operate in the United States, and what crimes do they engage in? Anonymous Witness. Yes, Senator. We have developed information that the following Russian organized crime groups have established their ties in several major metropolitan areas in the United States. They are the Izmailovskaya organization, the Solntsevskaya organization, the Chechen criminal organization, the Taganskaya criminal organization, and there are others that are still under investigation.

Senator ROTH. Now, as a typical example of Russian organized criminal activity, you described the extortion of a Russian business- man who, after he is threatened and his business vandalized, decides to pay. If he were to ask you, "What should I have done?" how would you have answered him?

Anonymous Witness. Senator, that is an extremely difficult question to answer. As a law enforcement officer, I would suggest that the businessman should file a complaint with the appropriate law enforcement agency. However, putting myself in the position of the Russian businessman, and understanding the limitation of law enforcement to protect the individual and his family on a continuing basis, I would suggest that he peacefully resolve this matter by cooperating with those who approached him.

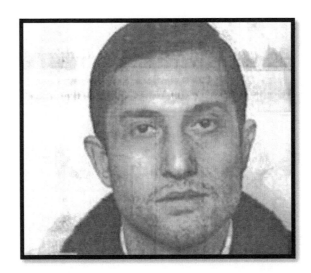

Senator ROTH. So in other words, to put it briefly, as a friend, you would tell him to pay?

Anonymous Witness. Right.

Senator ROTH. Let me ask you this question. You have been a police officer, as I understand it, for several years in this country.

Anonymous Witness. More than 15.

Senator ROTH. How do you see the activities of the Russian criminal groups changing over that period of years?

Anonymous Witness. It is becoming well-organized, well-funded; they are operating with huge amounts of money. They are becoming more and more sophisticated.

Senator ROTH. In other words, they are becoming more structured, better organized — more effective?

Anonymous Witness. More effective and integrated into the American business community.

Senator ROTH. Do you see them investing in a major way in legitimate businesses?

Anonymous Witness. Yes, Senator.

Senator ROTH. Let me ask all of you officers this question. You are the first line of defense against Russian organized crime. Are you satisfied with the level of cooperation you are receiving from State and Federal agencies? Mr. Mackey?

Mr. Mackey. Chairman ROTH, as a representative of the New York City Police Department, I can honestly say that although interagency cooperation does exist, there is certainly need for improvement.

We have had homicide investigations stymied because of parallel investigations involving the New York City Police Department and other agencies, where we are interested in solving a homicide, and they have their own agenda, and the forthrightness or the passing on of information did not occur in certain situations, which left us frustrated and unable to get certain goals accomplished. So we certainly need to address that problem and get some egos out of the way and get some major agency heads to sit down and actually, instead of making promises, to actually put some bite into what they are referring to and get things done, because without this cooperation on the Federal level and the State level and the local level, this is a crime problem that as representatives of local police departments, we cannot take on by ourselves.

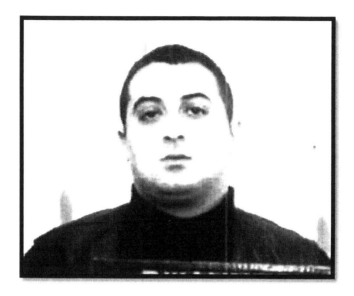

Senator ROTH. I suppose it is even accentuated by the fact that not only are they involved at the local level, but you have the international aspects of these criminal elements as well. But I think you make a very valid point and one that gives me real concern.

Mr. Mackey. Chairman ROTH, there were certainly a lot of promises made in this room today, and I certainly hope that a lot of these representatives from these different agencies come through on these promises.

Senator ROTH. Well, we will try to help to make sure they do in fact follow through, because you are exactly right; it is going to take cooperation at all levels of Government.

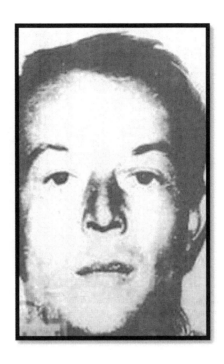

Mr. Mackey. Thank you, Mr. Chairman.

Senator ROTH. Mr. Cefarello?

Mr. Cefarello. Yes, I agree that some of the investigations have been stymied by Federal and city people not getting along or not sharing information. However, like I said in my statement, there are meetings held regularly with ourselves and Customs, INS, the State organized crime task force and all of these Federal agencies getting together with us, and we are doing fairly well at sharing information. I hope that in the case of the Resnikov killing and other killings that Mr. Casso spoke about, maybe we will get a shot at talking to him and finding out about some homicides he is speaking of; maybe he can help us clear them up. Maybe a Federal agency can help in that way.

Senator ROTH. Mr. Pollard?

Mr. Pollard. Mr. Chairman, at the present time, I enjoy a real good rapport with State and Federal agencies in all aspects through our meetings and our joint ventures as far as putting cases together and even the task force. I think everybody is pretty well aware of the problems and that we have to work together. In the Los Angeles area, most agencies are working together to try to get a handle on this.

Senator ROTH. Let me finally turn to our anonymous witness. Do you have any comment?

Anonymous Witness. Yes, Chairman. I can only speak for the area of the country in which I am currently working. Although we have an informal cooperation between several Federal, State and local law enforcement agencies, I would like to see full-time task forces established in which all of the appropriate agencies will con- tribute the necessary resources and effort to combat this growing problem. In my opinion, no one agency can accomplish this task alone.

Senator ROTH. You have a Russian background. Do you have any suggestions as to how to improve cooperation and exchange with the Russian authorities?

Anonymous Witness. Yes, Chairman. I would like to see a liaison established between the law enforcement agencies and the Russian communities in major metropolitan areas. I would like to see encouragement from the law enforcement agencies with the Russian communities to join the law enforcement agencies.

Senator ROTH. Thank you. Senator Nunn?

Senator NUNN. Thank you, Mr. Chairman. I had it in my opening statement, as I believe you did in yours, Mr. Chairman, but I would like to ask the police officers directly. We talk about Russian organized crime, but it sounds to me as if you are describing a much broader geographical description to include most of the former Soviet Union and even Eastern Europe. Would it be fair to say that, or are you really talking about Russia in a limited geographic sense? Could I ask our anonymous witness first?

Anonymous Witness. Yes, Senator. When I am referring to Russian organized crime, I am referring to the former Soviet Union republics.

Senator Nunn. The whole array, including Ukraine, Kazakhstan, Central Asia

Anonymous Witness. All 15 republics.

Senator NUNN. Are you also including Eastern Europe?

Anonymous Witness. Yes, Senator— Poland, former Czechoslovakia.

Senator Nunn. So as you use the word "Russian" here, it is a very broad description of, really, the former Soviet empire, is that right?

Anonymous Witness. You are right. Senator. The reason I am referring to "Russian organized crime" is because they all speak Russian, although they come from different republics.

Senator Nunn. So the common denominator is speaking the Russian language.

Anonymous Witness. Right.

Senator Nunn. Mr. Mackey?

Mr. Mackey. I concur. Senator Nunn, with my comrade — correction, my counterpart; I got carried away there — I concur with my counterpart regarding his testimony. As previously indicated, the phrase "Russian organized crime" is a misnomer, but for simplicity. it makes things a lot easier. But as indicated, we are also encountering Azerbaijanis, Armenians, Georgians, Chechens — a whole gamut of people from the former Soviet Union — in Brighton Beach.

Senator NUNN. Mr. Pollard, I cannot see you, but I think you can hear me.

Mr. Pollard. Yes, sir.

Senator Nunn. Do you concur in that, or do you have a different view?

Mr. Pollard. Yes, Senator, we concur as far as most of the Russian-speaking people. In the Los Angeles area, with the large population of Armenians, we do separate them out, and although they work together with the rest of the Russians, they have their own community, and it is large enough that we have a team that works on Armenians, and my partner and myself work on the rest of the Russians.

Senator Nunn. I would like to have an opinion from each of you, including our anonymous witness, as to how you compare the "Russian" or former Soviet Union organized crime problem in your communities with other organized crime, including traditional organized crime, the LCN, the Medellin cartel, the Jamaican posse, the various gangs that we have seen, the Crips, Bloods and so forth in Los

Angeles. As a general question, how do you compare the degree of bad influence, destruction, crime and so forth carried out by the Russian organized criminals compared to these other groups? Mr. Mackey?

Mr. Mackey. Senator Nunn, that certainly is a big sphere to address. We know that in New York City, as in other large cities where we had traditional organized crime or La Cosa Nostra in place, that the Federal Government and local governments have certainly been very, very effective in taking down their empires, certainly in the last couple of years.

We do have the cartels in place in New York City involved in narcotics, which are being addressed by different units of the police department, and the Jamaican posses as well. I am speaking here solely about Russian organized crime.

It certainly has the ability and the potential to become a serious threat to New York City if not checked in the near future. It certainly has the ability to move its tentacles out into the surrounding tri-State area as well.

Senator NUNN. Would it compare with the LCN now that the LCN has been knocked down in some particular families and so forth, and with the successes we have had? Which would be more serious now — the "Russian" organized crime problem in the New York area or the LCN?

Mr. Mackey. I would have to agree with other members of my profession that certainly LCN has the capability and has been involved in more activity. But with the vacuum recently created by the major take-downs of LCN families and people within their organization, Russian organized crime, again as a misnomer, is certainly standing by and ready to fill that vacuum if we are not there to take on this situation.

Senator NUNN. So LCN would still be more potent now, but you think the potential is there for Russian organized crime to step into the vacuum that is being created?

Mr. Mackey. Yes. I certainly do not feel there is anyone in the room who would state that the LCN or traditional organized crime has been completely decimated by law enforcement. We know that they still exist; however, we have been chipping away strongly over the past couple of years and making great inroads. But again, as I stated, the Russian organized crime — certainly, it is vying for power and it is out there, and we have got to get it in check soon.

Senator Nunn. How about in Los Angeles, Mr. Pollard, the same question — how does this compare relative to other organized criminal activities including LCN, but also including organizations like the Crips and the Bloods that we have had hearings on before here?

Mr. Pollard. Yes, Senator. First of all, addressing the Crips and Bloods and some of the others, that is a major problem that we probably have more violence from than most of the rest of the groups put together in terms of drive-by shootings and that type of activity. That is being addressed by several

170

different divisions and groups within my department. In terms of other ethnic groups, there are several around, none of which seem to have the potential at this point that I can see that the Russians do — and I use that term "Russian" including Armenians in this sense.

Senator Nunn. Right.

Mr. Pollard. The LCN in Los Angeles has never been as strong as the East Coast LCN. In fact, they have terms for themselves that include "Mickey Mouse Mafia" and things like that, that show that

Senator Nunn. "Mickey Mouse" what?

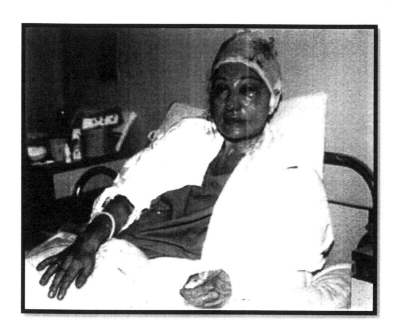

Anna Zarkova, award-winning crime reporter, had sulfuric acid hurled in her face by the Russian Mob.

Mr. Pollard. They refer to themselves even as the "Mickey Mouse Mafia" on the West Coast, and they do not seem to have the strength of any of the families from the East Coast. East Coast families come out and set up businesses and do not even contact them for approval or to pay tribute. So the LCN is not that strong of an issue in the Los Angeles area. I personally believe — and it is probably because I am working the Russians — that the Russians have a little more power right now and are going to be a lot more powerful as things progress.

Senator Nunn. Could I ask our undercover police officer the same question? In general, comparing this group that we have called for the purposes of this hearing "Russian organized crime" to other organized criminal activities in the area of your expertise?

Anonymous Witness. Senator, I consider myself an export on Russian organized crime. I am not familiar with the other — or, I was not involved in the other criminal organization investigations. So I would have to accept the opinion of my comrade from New York as well as my colleagues from other cities.

Senator Nunn. You are accepting him as a comrade, right?

Anonymous Witness. Yes, Senator.

Senator Nunn. OK. I would like to ask our witnesses from New York and L.A. this question. You have heard the undercover witness here basically say that he would have to advise someone who was being extorted in this situation to cooperate rather than to go to the police officials. Would that be, in your area, also your view, or do you have a different position?

Mr. Cefarello. I believe that at this time, I would probably have to tell somebody the same thing that he is saying. It is probably a lot safer right now to just pay the money. However, as a law enforcement officer, I do not want to do some-thing like that. What I would suggest is that we find a way to protect this person's family here and in the former Soviet Union.

Senator NUNN. You are saying you need a lot better protection for people who come to the law enforcement officials with those kinds of complaints than we have now.

Mr. Cefarello. Right. Right now, we have the witness protection program. That helps for the person who is talking here. What about his wife or his child or his mother and father in Russia, whom we cannot protect at this time and are vulnerable?

Senator Nunn. Do you concur in that, Mr. Mackey?

Mr. Mackey. I disagree, Senator Nunn, only because I would probably get my head lopped off if I went back and stated anything to the contrary. Any complainant who walks into a New York City police precinct, we certainly have to entertain and accept every complaint that is given to us, and we would certainly advise any complainant coming in who was the victim of an attempted extortion or an extortion that we are there, willing and able to provide the assistance and conduct the investigation to possibly arrest and then probably prosecute these people — although, as stated earlier, it is very, very difficult to get past the arrest stage with these people. A lot of them are very, very happy in the NYPD vernacular to "take the collar," and then once the "collar" is over, never show up for grand jury proceedings or any further prosecution.

Senator Nunn. Mr. Pollard, could I ask you to answer the same question — extortion and your advice in L.A. to potential or actual victims?

Mr. Pollard. Yes, Senator. In Los Angeles, I try to get every victim I can who is reporting an extortion to actively go along with our investigation. The biggest problem we have after that point is with the prosecutors. We are having to educate individual prosecutors as we go with particular cases, and this is a problem because in large cities, the prosecutors have a filing policy that unless it meets a certain level, they are not going to prosecute the case. A lot of our cases fall below that level. We need to prosecute every case we can, and that does two things. It sends a message to the criminals that our system is not going to allow their activities, but it also sends a message to the Russian-speaking community that we are there, and we can help them. And without getting into that community, we are never going to have them come forward again.

Senator Nunn. Thank you, Mr. Pollard. You are the "anonymous witness" as far as I am concerned, since I cannot see you, but we appreciate you being here. Mr. Cefarello, Mr. Mackey, and our undercover police officer, we thank all of you for being here, and Senator ROTH, to you and your staff, thank you for having the focus on this. I think it is a very important subject, and I congratulate you for the hearing and the focus.

Senator ROTH. Thank you, Senator Nunn. I want to thank each of you gentlemen for being here. I think your testimony has been most helpful.

For the final time, I will ask that the Capitol Police secure the hearing room, ensure that all spectators remain seated, and that no one be allowed to enter or leave the hearing room during this witness' exit.

Prior to the exit of this witness, I direct that all cameras be turned to face either to the rear or to the window side of the hear- ing room. I understand the cameras have all been turned, and I would ask that the witness now leave the hearing room. Again, I want to thank each of you. We do not want any of your heads lopped off.

The Subcommittee is in recess.

[Whereupon, at 1:50 p.m., the Subcommittee was adjourned.]

Written statement of the City of Glendale, California Police Department

Dear Senators:

The City of Glendale, California Police Department regrets that it cannot make available a law enforcement representative to personally testify before the subcommittee as we had originally planned. But we do hope that our voice can still be heard by submitting this document so that it may be introduced into the subcommittee record as to our efforts in attempting to thwart the Armenian and Russian Armenian organized crime problem.

Historically, Glendale has been a homogenous community made up predominantly of Caucasian population. The city for years was considered a middle to upper middle class conservative neighborhood. However, approximately twenty-five years ago the demographics of the city began to change and Glendale became a heterogeneous community. The influx of the Armenian population to the Glendale area, specifically Russian Armenian, is attributed to two waves of migration. In the early 1980's, we saw the first wave of migration of the Russian Armenians to the Glendale and adjoining cities. Then, in 1991, after the fall of the "Iron Curtain", the City of Glendale experienced a drastic population increase within the Russian Armenian communities. Currently, the city's population is estimated at 200,000, of which is roughly 25% Armenian. It is estimated that approximately 50% of the city's Armenian population is Russian Armenian.

To meet the demands of the cultural diversity of the city, the police department began an aggressive recruiting effort to balance its work force to meet the demands of the community. At present, the Glendale Police Department employs 223 sworn personnel, and upwards of 10 civilian employees. Of these employees, we have (4) full time Armenian police officers and (6) civilian Armenian employees. This translates into roughly 3.5% of the work force having an Armenian background. In addition, the Glendale Police Department has (4) reserve police officers of Armenian descent, and upon successful completion of the police academy, we will soon be adding a Russian speaking officer to full time status.

In 1994, the management of the Glendale Police Department realized there was significant Russian Armenian organized crime developing within the city as well as throughout the region of Los Angeles County. As a result, the Glendale Police Department expanded its criminal intelligence unit to also include an organized crime unit. With limited manpower and resources, the department allocated a sergeant and three officers to address the organized crime issues of the Russian Armenian communities not only in Glendale, but throughout the region.

At present, our criminal intelligence and organized crime unit investigates and gathers information on crimes against persons, crimes against property, fraud related crime and narcotic offenses. Of these, our unit along with the assistance of other units of the department, investigate murders, extortions, robberies, felonious assaults, arsons. Financial crimes including, money laundering, check kiting, counterfeit check production, auto insurance/medical insurance fraud, electronic fraud (credit card fraud and cellular phone fraud). Additionally Glendale has always been aggressively involved with enforcing narcotic smuggling and distribution.

The following is a synopsis of three investigations which directly involve Russian Armenian organized crime elements in the Glendale and surrounding areas.

1) Murders with in the garment district:

-A multi-agency cooperative effort has been established to investigate the recent rash of violent murders and attempted murders associated with the garment district, which are primarily Russian-Armenian owned businesses. Intelligence gathering revealed a major clothing line had sub-contracted out to several sweat-shops to reduce production costs in the Los Angeles and Glendale areas. As a result, stiff competition came about as sub-contractors attempted to underbid in order to obtain the production contract. In some instances, there were bribes and "kickbacks" to company management in order to leave a contract with a certain subcontractor. Sub-contractors became disgruntled and the garment district wars began. To date, there have been five murders, five attempted murders, shootings, bombings and extortions committed within the garment district. All of these incidents are believed to be organized crime related since due to clear indications that sub-contractors were tied very closely to organized crime figures and known hit-men. As a result of these crimes, there has been one conviction for murder.

2) Extortions:

- This agency conducted an extortion investigation where an individual, Hagop Kerboyan was extorting money from a Glendale chiropractic doctor. Threats were made to force the doctor to pay a substantial amount of money in lieu of physical injury. It was later determined the doctor was committing insurance fraud on the State of California for large sums of money. Kerboyan, having knowledge of this extorted the doctor, believing because he was conducting a fraudulent business, would not report the extortion. Ultimately Kerboyan was convicted and the doctor was indicted. Our investigation has also revealed that Kerboyan belongs to a organized crime cell in the Glendale area.

Investigating these types of cases indicates that although up until now, the Russian Armenian criminals were not structured as traditional Italian organized crime, but they are becoming increasingly structured and disciplined. It is evident that there are cells of loosely structured groups which contain anywhere from ten to one hundred individuals. These groups have agreed to divide the Los Angeles region into territories which are controlled by their respective criminal groups. These groups extort "territory taxes" from the businesses within their specific area.

If businesses refuse to pay, they usually are threatened often resulting in murder. Their family members are also threatened in order to send a message. In some cases, family members are threatened who live in their former homeland (usually Armenia) if they do not cooperate. Due to the threatened violence, the victims are forced to pay the extortionists, and thus the crimes go unreported. These criminal groups have become increasingly educated in their criminal activities in that they are now targeting victims that are medical professionals and lawyers who themselves are engaged in medical insurance fraud or auto insurance fraud, (staged auto collisions). The extortion groups know that this group of individuals are less likely to report the extortions to law enforcement due to their own involvement in criminal activity and the large financial return. Often times the results of these extortions are shootings, stabbings, and murder.

3) White collar crime and electronic fraud:

-These crimes include check counterfeiting and kiting, money laundering, cellular phone fraud, and credit card fraud. Of particular interest is a case in which a Russian Armenian had been cloning cellular phones for over three years. He had been arrested for a previous cellular phone fraud offense and was on probation when our investigation began. Through our investigations, we learned that the subject of our investigation was cloning the cellular phones of the "Joe Mikaelyan" crime group.

This crime group was recently dismantled by a joint task force which was made up of the Federal Bureau of Investigation, the Internal Revenue Service, Long Beach Police Department, Los Angeles Police Department and the California Department of Justice. Joe Mikaelyan, a self-professed Armenian Mafia Godfather, and his crime group were responsible for financial losses that reached multi-million dollar figures as it related to tax evasion, cellular phone cloning and fraud related crimes. Our investigation revealed that Joe Mikaelyan routinely telephoned and received calls from top-level Russian crime figures located on the east coast.

The suspect in our cellular phone cloning operation had been under investigation by the cellular phone industry for several years. The cellular phone industry estimates that in North America, more than $600,000,000 annually are lost in revenue due to cellular phone cloning and related expenses for investigations into their losses.

The leading states for cellular phone fraud are New York, Florida, and California. The cellular phone industry believes the Russian Armenians to not only be the "Godfathers" of cellular phone fraud, but also the leaders in cellular phone cloning, and responsible for the vast majority of their losses. The cellular phone industries representatives further explained that no other criminal group has dominated the illegal cellular phone cloning operations the way the Russian Armenian community has. While investigating a cellular phone cloning suspect, we learned that in a one month period he was responsible for a loss in excess of $140,000 to the cellular phone companies. This translates into an annual loss of over 1.6 million

dollars.

Recently, the Glendale Police organized crime unit investigated two Russian Armenian Brothers who had developed a process to defraud not only the cellular phone companies, but also long distance telephone carriers such as ATT and MCI.

The two suspects had printed business cards advertising 24 hour service for long distance calling to countries around the world. The business cards were printed in Russian and Armenian languages, thereby operating under a comfort zone and screening customers. The two suspects had set up a bank of three pairs of cloned cellular phones, having phones linked to each other. In order to speak to friends and relatives overseas, particularly in Russia and Armenia, the customer phoned the beeper number on the business card. Once the call was completed, the suspect would send a "runner" to the customer's residence to collect the money for the phone call. Although these crimes may seem to be less significant in the realm of more serious and violent crimes, they are an indication as to how complex some investigations can be when dealing with fraudulent crime.

Compared to traditional organized crime, we have learned that the criminals we investigate tend to be more opportunistic then organized. An accurate description of these groups is loosely structured organized cells of criminal groups. However, this does not diminish the organized and violent manner in which they commit their crimes. It is our opinion, that we are witnessing the precursors to the traditional organized crime "family" structures with bosses, captains, lieutenants, and field soldiers. If this does occur, prosecution of top level figures would be difficult.

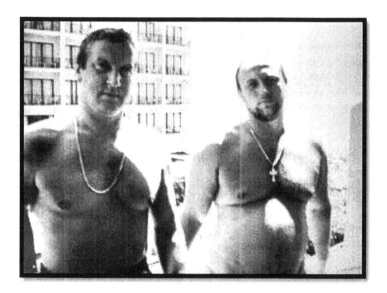

The following factors make it difficult for law enforcement to attack the Russia /Russian Armenian organized crime problems within the Los Angeles and Glendale regions:

-the lack of Russian or Armenian speaking investigators;

-the language barriers under which these criminals operate, which has become their comfort zone;

-the ability for Russian criminals to operate so well in a black market setting, due their past ability to survive in a communist economy in their homelands;

-their lack of fear or respect for the American Judicial System because of their knowledge of the leniency of the courts due to overcrowding of jails and prisons;

-their propensity towards violence due to their background and upbringing;
-the ability for Russian or Armenian foreigners to enter the country illegally or with "tourist" visas to commit a specific crime, which often times means an extortion or gangland murder. Soon after they commit their crimes, they flee the country only to return some years later with different identities;

-the sophisticated manner in which criminal activity is carried out within the Russian and Russian Armenian criminal groups. This again can be directly attributable to the fact that they come from a system where criminal activity is common place;

-the educational and training background of these organized crime members, some of whom have been former KGB agents, former police officers, politicians, medical professionals and such back in their countries.

As an example, several years ago our department arrested the former police chief of the city of Yerevan, Armenia's capital, for an investigation into extortion, rape, and kidnapping;

-and finally, the loose structuring of these criminal groups makes it difficult for law enforcement to track criminal activity and identify co-conspirators.

In conclusion, it is our opinion that crime associated with the Russian and Russian Armenian communities will become more violent, sophisticated, and clandestine. Law enforcement today is ill equipped to effectively investigate the issues of Russian organized crime. Although addressing the issues is a positive step, law enforcement is in need of the tools to apply intelligence information to actual investigations and subsequent arrests. This includes additional manpower, equipment, and a multi-agency joint task force comprised of federal, state, and local resources. Task forces are effective means to target Russian organized crime before establishing an irreversible foothold in the United States, as- traditional organized crime. For smaller agencies, it is difficult to allocate significant amounts of resources to combat Russian organized crime. However, if the resources of smaller agencies are combined with resources of larger agencies, the results will be far more effective.

Tariel Oniani

STATEMENT OF EDWARD L. FEDEWCO, Jr.
DIRECTOR, NATIONAL OPERATIONS, CRIMINAL INVESTIGATION
INTERNAL REVENUE SERVICE
BEFORE THE PERMANENT SUBCOMMITTEE ON INVESTIGATIONS
SENATE COMMITTEE ON GOVERNMENTAL AFFAIRS
MAY 15, 1996

Good Morning Mr. Chairman and distinguished members of the subcommittee. I appreciate the opportunity to be here today to discuss the internal Revenue Service Criminal Investigation Division's experience with organized crime from the former Soviet Union (FSU).

I would like to highlight a significant point that illustrates the impact of financial investigations — AND the expertise of IRS Criminal Investigation special agents - on combating organized crime. Nearly everyone has heard of Al Capone, but what you may not know is that while many federal and state agencies attempted to prosecute Capone for everything from murder to bootlegging, it took an IRS special agent working undercover to obtain information that allowed IRS to unravel Capone 's books and ledgers and to painstakingly build an airtight case against him. America's most infamous gangster was found guilty and sent to prison for income tax evasion.

Capone

The Capone investigation was certainly not our largest or most complex investigation; however, it is a perfect example of what we do. When more conventional investigative techniques fail, we follow the money trail — the proceeds of crime eventually lead to the criminal. IRS special agents have been doing this for over 77 years.

Waxy Gordon

Some of the most notable organized crime figures who could not hide from the reaches of the IRS were figures such as one of Capone' s henchmen, Waxey Gordon who was sentenced in 1932 to 10 years in prison for tax evasion; John Gotti who was sentenced in 1 990 to life in prison - among the charges on which he was convicted was a Klein conspiracy, which means he attempted to impede and defeat the lawful collection of income taxes for the years 1984-1989; Rocco Infelise, Chicago's crime boss who was sentenced in 1 993 to 63 years in prison for running a bookmaking operation; in February of this year, Anthony (Fat Tony) Morelli, who was sentenced to 20 years for his prominent role in the Red Daisy diesel fuel scheme in Newark; and Chicago's 74 year old mobster Samuel Carlisi who was sentenced in March 1996 to 1 51 months in prison for failure to pay wagering taxes.

Gotti

Rocco Infelise

Carlisi

What IRS Does Best Since our inception as the law enforcement arm of the Internal Revenue Service, we have always known that greed is the powerful motivation behind the crimes we investigate. The crimes we investigate, like the greed itself, are found in all strata of our society. Whenever greed leads to crime, whether income tax evasion or international money laundering. Criminal Investigation is involved. Our investigations take us to corporate board rooms as well as to crack houses. IRS Criminal Investigation special agents fill a unique niche in the law enforcement community, that of financial investigators. The special agent's accounting and law enforcement skills are essential qualities in conducting investigations which have led to the conviction of high profile criminals who commit increasingly sophisticated financial crimes. The success of our investigations enhances voluntary compliance by increasing confidence with the federal tax system and deterring others from engaging in similar conduct. Criminal Investigation also cooperates closely with other government agencies to investigate criminal activity. The Bank Secrecy Act, the Money Laundering Control Act and the provisions of Title 26 of the United States Code outline the role and responsibilities of the IRS Criminal Investigation Division in investigations that cross agency boundaries. Thus, our investigations cover not only white collar crime but also crimes involving illegal industry.

For example, drug dealers have been going to jail for years for the illegal distribution of narcotics; however, at IRS, we pursue drug dealers not for the drugs but for their unreported income and for laundering their illegal profits. By focusing our investigations on the "kingpins" of narcotics, we expend our scarce resources on the high dollar, high impact investigations where the nation's taxpayers will get the "biggest bang for their buck." By taking away the thing they prize most, their money, we are shutting down the drug kingpin's money laundering capabilities and ultimately stopping the flow of narcotics onto our streets and neighborhoods.

 What IRS Knows About Organized Crime To combat organized crime one must have a thorough understanding of the criminals involved. This has been particularly true of our efforts to combat motor fuel excise tax evasion schemes that have been perpetrated by organized crime, and especially by organized crime from the former Soviet Union.

We have identified some significant characteristics of individuals involved in these newly established criminal enterprises.

• They display a remarkable aptitude for sophisticated white collar crime. They are mostly well educated, many having advanced university degrees in mathematics, economics and the sciences. They are adept at functioning in a black market economy and they are skilled at corrupting members of a targeted industry, in this instance, fuel whole sale distributors and retailers.

• They are ruthless, employing threats, intimidation and violence to further their aims. The Russians have a long history of settling disputes in the Brighton Beach, New York area by resorting to murder. Two of the more infamous were the 1989 slayings of Michael Markowitz and Phillip Moskowitz, two major players in many motor fuel bootlegging schemes. IRS agents, working in undercover roles, received many threats during the investigation. Threats of violence were delivered in person or by phone, and in other instances funeral wreaths were sent to our undercover offices inscribed "Rest in Peace." During the motor fuel excise tax evasion investigation called "Red Daisy," our undercover offices were set on fire and burned after our undercover agents failed to heed warnings to stop competing with mob-controlled firms.

NOTE ON THE TEXT: In 1986, Joseph "Joe Glitz" Galizia (July 24, 1941–1998) a ranking member of the Genovese Family and Michael Franzese, and their Russian partners were charged with evading over $5 million in taxes in just a few months. All the defendants were eventually convicted or plead guilty and went to federal prison. In 1989, while in prison, Galizia was suspected by federal investigators for being involved in ordering the murder of Michael Markowitz, a Russian gangster who flipped. Markowitz was shot to death in Brooklyn by Joseph Reisch. Galizia would be indicted again on similar charges in 1991. A hood described Markowitz as "one of the bigger bootleggers in the New York area. He was an eastern bloc immigrant who came to this country with virtually no money in 1979 but at the time of his death had "upwards of 30 million dollars just in assets... not even counting various bank accounts over in Austria and Lichtenstein." Markowitz was shot in the head while sitting in his Rolls Royce in Brooklyn in 1989. Phillip Moskowitz was murdered after he was indicted and "certain tapes were released in which he compromised the positions of various organized crime families and identified them as being active in the bootlegging business. His body was found in New Jersey,"

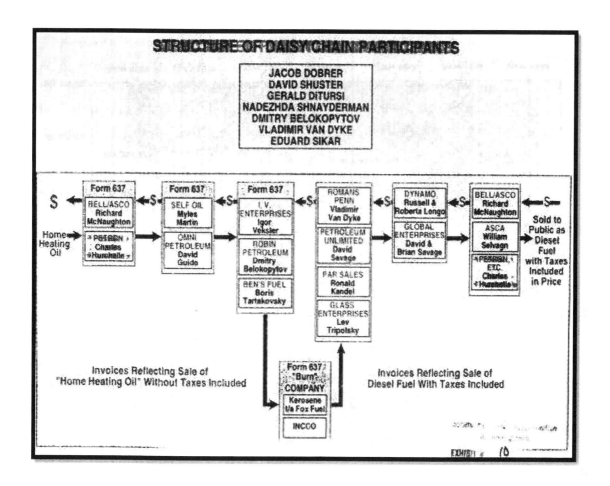

STRUCTURE OF DAISY CHAIN PARTICIPANTS

JACOB DOBRER
DAVID SHUSTER
GERALD DITURSI
NADEZHDA SHNAYDERMAN
DMITRY BELOKOPYTOV
VLADIMIR VAN DYKE
EDUARD SIKAR

• They are highly adaptable. They work easily with various ethnic groups and show a willingness to "cut others in" if there is a profit margin for them or if it will further their enterprises. For example, oil dealer Charles Hurchalla, of Exton, Pennsylvania, selflessly agreed to allow the government to use his business and act as an undercover agent in the $14.8 million Philadelphia investigation. To gain his cooperation, the Russians presented him with a gold Rolex President watch worth $15,000 as a bonus or business incentive. During the course of the investigation the criminals suspected that Hurchaila was acting as a government agent, so they summoned him to a meeting in New York City to confront him. They ended up offering him a more lucrative cut of the profits. Hurchaila advised the IRS that "the Russians believe that everyone has their price and with enough money almost anyone, whether in government or private industry, can be corrupted." According to our informants, if this approach does not work, the Russians have a "join up or die" strategy.

• They are not monopolistic; they are fluid. Their structure is different from traditional organized crime. We have observed that a group of Russians may band together to devise and execute a particular scheme and continue in that mode until they are either stopped by law enforcement or until something better comes along. There may be a leader of the scheme but there does not seem to be an organizational hierarchy which continues beyond that particular group. This has been particularly true in the motor fuel excise tax schemes.

Motor Fuel Excise Tax Evasion

What started out as a novel fraud scheme contrived by a fuel retailer in Long Island to steal federal and state gasoline taxes quickly evolved into a serious noncompliance problem resulting in the loss of more than "$1 billion" in revenue annually. Initially, gasoline was the product of choice.

Gasoline is sold at thousands of retail locations, and gasoline excise tax revenues constitute almost 70 percent of the approximately $20 billion in motor fuel taxes collected annually.

To give you an idea of the money involved, an average tanker truck holds 8 thousand gallons of fuel. The combined federal and state taxes per gallon of fuel can exceed 40 cents. So, the average tax per tanker is $3,200. The complicated "bootleg" or "daisy chain' schemes, devised by the Russians, puts that $3,200 per tanker into their pockets instead of the US Treasury. When one considers that a large scheme can move 10 to 70 loads of fuel per day, the losses can be staggering! This revenue that could have been used to build and maintain our national transportation systems and infrastructure is stolen. These stolen revenues have enriched traditional organized crime families and furnished the means by which "Russian" organized criminal elements initially consolidated and ultimately expanded the scope of their sinister activities in the United States.

To say that these bootleg and daisy chain schemes are complicated, well planned, well organized operations would be an understatement! Yet they can be unraveled. We have been doing that successfully for over 10 years. To briefly demonstrate the complexity of these schemes, the following are some examples of daisy chain and a bootleg-type operations.

Daisy Chain

A daisy chain scheme is the method which was developed by organized crime expressly for the purpose of stealing federal and state fuel excise tax revenues. Daisy chains are schemes that capitalized on weaknesses in our motor fuel excise tax laws. In the typical daisy chain operation, a complex paper trail of motor fuel transactions is created. At some point along the chain, the sale is fictitiously invoiced as tax-paid fuel, but the company supposedly claiming to have paid the tax turns out to be a fictitious entity, or an entity with no assets called a "burn" company. By the time auditors and investigators unravel the series of transactions to determine the tax liability, the so-called "bum" company has disappeared without a trace of records or assets.

For such an operation to work, the perpetrator must be able to purchase fuel tax-free. In the case of the federal excise tax, this means having a registration number assigned by the IRS on Form 637, Certification of Exemption. Legitimate registration numbers have been obtained for fraudulent purposes by buying out registered companies or falsifying documents of legitimate companies.

The Newark investigation we called "Red Daisy" was an ambitious undercover operation that exposed organized crime influence in the fuel business in New York, New Jersey and Pennsylvania organized and executed by Russian emigres under the protection of mob boss Anthony (Fat Tony) Morelli. The first phase of this multi-part, two year investigation focused on a scheme which defrauded the federal and state governments of $60 million in fuel excise taxes. In this scheme, members of the Russian "Mafia" paid tribute to members of New York organized crime families including Mafia godfather, John Gotti. Over 100 million gallons of fuel were sold. The scope of this operation, its inherent complexity and risks involved were daunting.

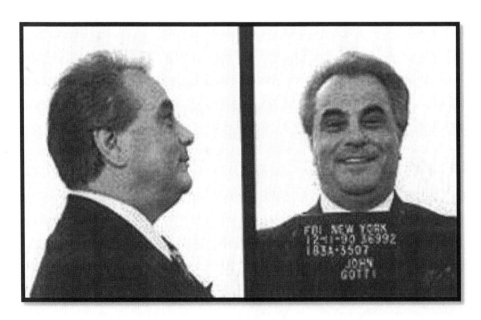

Gotti

During the course of this investigation, hundreds of meetings and over 1200 telephone conversations were recorded and transcribed. Surveillances were conducted for months and the documentary evidence filled a 1,000 square foot storage area. As the investigation progressed, our undercover agents became so influential in the bootleg fuel industry that mobsters warned them to join their operation, get out of the business, or suffer the consequences. This threat became reality when the building being operated by the undercover agents was burned to the ground.

In spite of the dangers involved, the Red Daisy was a great success. As of this date all defendants have been convicted. Moreover, on August 8, 1995, the second phase of the Red Daisy indictment was announced by a grand jury. This indictment charged 25 corrupt fuel dealers, along with members of both traditional and organized crime from the former Soviet Union, with the theft of over $140 million in federal motor fuel excise tax revenue. This case, currently awaiting trial, is the largest tax evasion case in history.

In Atlanta, our IRS agents unraveled a complicated daisy chain scheme whereby Russians attempted to establish themselves in Georgia. Michael Vax, Ilia Miller and eight other defendants (mostly Russians) fraudulently obtained IRS Form 637 exemption certificates for the purpose of purchasing fuel tax free. They then constructed an elaborate series of daisy chain schemes to steal the excise taxes collected from retailers. They took careful steps to conceal their criminal enterprise, including the creation of double sets of financial records and structuring cash transactions to buy fuel for their bootleg business and return cash to co-conspirators which enabled them to launder their profits. During this investigation, the criminal enterprise sold over 6,000,000 gallons of diesel and 130,500 gallons of gasoline and evaded $1.6 million in taxes. Vax and his co-conspirators were charged with racketeering (RICO) activity, money laundering and tax evasion. All were subsequently convicted. Vax received a 41 month prison sentence.

Bootleg Scheme

Bootlegging is a term which denotes any scheme to sell illegal or untaxed products. (This harks back to the days of prohibition when organized criminals sold bootleg liquor.) For the Russians, one of the ways in which they get untaxed fuel is by creating false Forms 637 and presenting them to wholesalers to dupe the wholesalers into selling them diesel fuel tax free.

In an IRS investigation in California called "Diesel Storm," Joseph Yosi Ezra and Leah Isaac pled guilty to their involvement in a scheme which stole almost $2 million in federal excise taxes in just two months. Using false Forms 637, the pair bought over 10 million gallons of diesel fuel tax free and sold it to dealers or at service stations which they owned, thereby giving themselves a competitive advantage so that they could sell their fuel at cheaper prices and still make a profit. These are just some of the schemes investigated around the country. Regardless of size, they dramatically illustrate the potential damage to our economy that can occur if these schemes go unchecked.

I must point out that fuel excise tax evasion hurts not only the federal and state governments by depriving them of revenue, but has a profound negative impact on legitimate fuel distributors and retailers as well. Their market shares erode, their profits decline and some are even forced out of business. Honest businessmen simply cannot compete with criminals.

The History of "Fuel"

In the 1980's, the major oil companies sold many of their brand name service stations and fuel terminals in the New York metropolitan area. Many were subsequently acquired by members of various immigrant groups, among them immigrants from the former Soviet Union. When the potential of motor fuel excise tax schemes was recognized by organized crime, the Russians were in an ideal position to sell bootleg gasoline at the stations they controlled.

Gasoline

During 1984-1988, gasoline schemes abounded - and they were large schemes which often took years to investigate using traditional methods. Further, no matter how many bootleggers we convicted, more stood ready to become involved in these schemes because the lure of illicit profits was simply too great. In 1988, legislative reforms moved the point of taxation on gasoline from the wholesale distributor level to the terminal rack. This change resulted in substantially improved compliance. Denied the ability to steal gasoline excise tax revenue, the Russians quickly began to organize instead diesel fuel evasion schemes. Because the demand for diesel fuel is much less than gasoline, the Russians were forced to expand their operations from New York into New Jersey, Pennsylvania, Georgia and Ohio, as well as other previously unaffected areas. The diesel fuel evasion problem worsened from 1 988 to 1 991 . We began to utilize ambitious, deep penetration undercover operations to address this problem, and we had tremendous success.

For example, over a two year period, beginning in June 1990, taxable gallons of diesel fuel reported declined in the State of Pennsylvania from 963,484,013 to 932,672,803. This drop in taxable gallons reported and the corresponding drop in revenue was almost totally attributable to the influence of organized crime. Beginning in March 1993 and continuing through August 1995, our undercover operations resulted in 10 major indictments. Collectively, these investigations are some of the most significant in the history of motor fuel prosecutions, involving 136 defendants and over $363 million in evaded taxes. Among these defendants are some of the highest ranking members of both traditional organized crime and organized crime from the former Soviet Union. To date, 99 defendants have pled guilty or have been convicted; the remaining 37 are awaiting trial. These cases are but a part of the 21 1 persons indicted for motor fuel excise tax evasion during the past three fiscal years.

These successful prosecutions, including that of the head of the Russian Mob in

New York, Morat Balagula, and organized crime boss Victor Orena, Jr., helped break the hold of organized crime on the retail fuel distribution industry in the New York metropolitan area.

Victor Orena

Dyed Fuel

In August 1993, Congress passed the Omnibus Budget Reconciliation Act of 1 993. The Act moved the point of taxation of diesel fuel from the wholesale distributor level to the terminal rack. Further, this legislation provided that only dyed fuel is exempt from tax after January 1 , 1 994 and that dyed fuel cannot be used on the highway. It must be used for off-road purposes such as for home heating or farm use.

These important legislative changes, supported by the fuel industry, revolutionized the situation by further reducing the opportunity for evasion. The implementation of diesel fuel dyeing was an important step. Formerly, fuel used for tax exempt purposes was not distinguishable from the taxed product. This made diversion of the product for illegal purposes a simple matter. Dyed fuel, by contrast, is exempt from tax, and because of its vivid red coloring, any attempted use of it on our highways can be readily discovered by the IRS Examination Division through the spot checking of terminals and tracks. This legislative remedy, however simple it may seem, has produced significant increases in compliance.

Revenue Enhancements

As a result of these important legislative changes and our investigative successes, federal diesel fuel receipts increased during calendar year 1994 by $1,765 billion. Of this increase, $681 million is attributable to the Diesel Compliance Initiative. State revenues across the nation have risen an average of almost 7 percent. In the worst affected states, this increase in revenue was almost 20 percent annually.

Cocktailed Fuel

So is the problem fixed? Not yet. The Russians are quite tenacious. Denied one avenue to evade taxes, they seek another. One of the current methods of evasion involves the blending and extending of the volume of taxable fuels. Good fuel is blended with nontaxed products such as kerosene, waste oil, toxic waste and other products into a mixture called "cocktailed fuel.' Excise taxes are not paid on the extended volume. This method of evasion extends the taxable fuel plus it takes care of the high costs of disposing of toxic waste. Criminals are selling these substandard and dangerous products to unsuspecting retail dealers and motorists in many parts of the country. This junk is clogging engines and even worse, it is polluting our air.

Another new scheme for the Russians involves purchasing taxed fuel (both federal and state taxes) in a low tax state such as New Jersey and shipping it to a high tax state such as New York. This simple scheme can result in up to a 1 2 cent per gallon advantage for the criminals in a business in which profit margins are ordinarily 2 to 3 cents per gallon. The State of New York estimates that this type of evasion scheme has cost them $20 million in revenue in the last 18 months. During 1994 and 1995, in Los Angeles, California, a group of Armenians and Russians made a concerted effort to dominate the independent fuel retailing industry by carrying out daisy chain evasion schemes to steal state excise tax revenues. Before the recent law changes, this group had previously evaded Federal diesel fuel taxes as well. On September 13, 1995, 15 members of this group were indicted for tax evasion, extortion, drug trafficking and the procurement of prostitutes from the former Soviet Union. Prior to indictment, this group had been actively experimenting with ways to defeat the new federal diesel fuel laws.

Despite the success we have had in combating motor fuel excise tax evasion schemes in the past, it would be naive to think that the Russians will simply abandon their efforts to steal motor fuel excise taxes. We believe they will continue to attempt to circumvent the law.

It should be noted that no matter how successful the government is in prosecuting motor fuel excise tax evaders, the Russians are so clever and persistent that only a comprehensive approach encompassing enforcement, regulation, legislative reform and close federal, state and industry cooperation can truly curtail their operations.

Since 1991, IRS has obtained over 190 convictions against many important members of organized crime and corrupt fuel dealers. The achievements in the fuel excise tax evasion area are the result of a collective effort and are a tribute to you and can be achieved when government and industry work together. I am proud of the role that the Internal Revenue Service, and Criminal Investigation in particular, has played in bringing about these successes.

Russian Mafia tattoos

The Future

We have studied the problems regarding organized crime from the former Soviet Union as it relates to motor fuel excise tax evasion. We have investigated their schemes. Congress has implemented significant legislative changes. As a result, we have seen crime in this area reduced.

I do not want to leave you with the impression that the IRS is only concerned about the effect of organized crime from the former Soviet Union on the fuel business. We have seen these groups branch out into some of the more "traditional" areas of crime. We now have IRS special agents actively involved in investigations regarding narcotics, health care fraud, insurance fraud, prostitution and diversion of assets earned in Russia from the sale of natural resources such as oil, timber, and diamonds.

As an example, in California, Russian émigré Michael Smushkevich was the mastermind of a medical diagnostic testing scheme that generated $1 billion of fraudulent billings to medical insurance carriers. Approximately $300 million was paid to the Smushkevich organization which was ultimately wired to foreign cities including Moscow. In September 1994, Smushkevich pled guilty to charges including money laundering and was sentenced to 21 years. The doctor who ran the clinics, Russian emigre Bogich Jovovich, also pled guilty to charges including money laundering and was sentenced to 20 years.

We recognize that the organized criminal element will not go away any time soon in America. But, we continue to stay on the paper trail of these organizations.

So, is the problem of organized crime from the former Soviet Union fixed? No. One means by which these criminal organizations might be more effectively combated in the future is through international cooperation.

Earlier in this statement, I made numerous observations about the Russians. Well, there is someone else who is also watching this group of organized criminals very closely - and they, too have concerns. They are the newly formed Russian

Government's national police, called the MVD, and the Russian Tax Police. We are joining forces with these officials in areas of mutual concern to create a formidable force that might just break and hopefully dissolve this threat of organized crime from the former Soviet Union.

Since March 1995, IRS has taught financial investigative techniques to over 350 law enforcement personnel from the Russian Federation of Tax Police, the Ukraine Ministry of Finance and state tax inspection police, the Ministry of Finance in Minsk, Belarus, and midlevel managers and criminal investigators of the Russian Tax Police in St. Petersburg, Russia. The student population ranges from the Assistant Minister of Finance, to the top Tax Police, to the Ministry of Internal Affairs, to regular tax police.

Additionally, a 12 hour course has been, and is continuing to be, taught by IRS special agents at the International Law Enforcement Academy in Budapest, Hungary. This academy is a State Department- sponsored program which has the full support of the IRS - in fact, IRS Commissioner Margaret Richardson participated in the dedication ceremonies of the academy in April of this year. Some of the course topics taught by IRS include Documentation and Evidence, Indicators of Financial Fraud, Money Laundering, and Methods of Proof.

Additionally, IRS is part of the assessment team which recently returned from Moscow. The team includes a representative from the Secret Service, the Federal Reserve, the Office of the Comptroller of the Currency, and the Federal Bureau of Investigation. The purpose of the team visit was to conduct a joint needs assessment for the Russian banking system with an eye to preventing fraud and money laundering. The recommendations include tighter banking regulations, new money laundering legislation, and training for law enforcement and the banking community.

During the recent visit to Moscow, the MVD and Tax Police requested that IRS assign a special agent to the Embassy in Moscow to assist and/or work jointly with them on investigations involving financial crimes and money laundering. In coordination with the U.S. Ambassador and the State Department, we are currently considering their invitation.

With continued vigilance, cooperation and legislative support such as I outlined here today, we can make great progress. Mr. Chairman, I will be happy to answer any questions you and the other subcommittee members may have.

Four groups that make up the Russian mafia

1. Elite group – led by a Pakhan who is involved in management, organization and ideology. This is the highest group controls both support group and security group.

2. Security group – is led by one of his spies. His job is to make sure the organization keeps running and also keeps the peace between the organizations and other criminal groups and also paying off the right people. This group works with the Elite group and is equal in power with the Support groups. Is in charge of security and in intelligence.

3. Support group- is led by one of his spies. His job is to watch over the working unit collecting the money while supervising their criminal actives. This group works with the elite group and is equal in power with the Security group. They plan a specific crime for a specialized group or choose who carries out the operation.

4. Working Unit – There are four Brigadiers running a criminal activity in the working unit. Each Brigade is controlled by a Brigadier. This is the lowest group working with only the Support group. The group is involved in burglars, thieves, prostitution, extortion, street gangs and other crimes.
In the Russian Mafia to become a "Vor" (plural: Vory) (a Thief) is an honorary title meaning to become a made man. The honor of becoming a Vor is only given when the recruit show's considerable leadership skills, personal ability, intellect and charisma. Pakhan or another high ranking member of an organization can decided if the recruit will receive such title. When you become a member amongst

the Vor-world you have accept the code Vor v Zakone or Thief inside the Law (compare to outlaws).

The Bratva (literally the Brotherhood), or so called Russian Mafia has a somewhat unorganized structure. There are only a few groups which are organized, but most of the other groups stays unorganized. To explain more, there's the leader who is called Pakhan (the Father), he has all the power and is in charge of everything. Pakhan questions everybody and no one questions his authority. Putting the Pakhan's word in question constitutes an automatic dispel out of the organization in the best case scenario which also can lead to the termination of the individual. Most of the regulations are based on certain understandings, traditions, and, of course, are not documented. One has to be cultured in the environment to learn all the understandings and traditions of certain criminal groups which vary in inconsiderable degree.

Beside Pakhan there is also a Councilor, called Sovietnik, which gives advices. Sovietniks are the most close and trusted individuals of Pakhan. Then the next rank is the Obshchak, which is a so called bookmaker in the Russian mafia, collects all money and bribes the government. The next rank is a Avtorityet (Authority), each avtorityet has earned its place, by proving himself to every other criminal, they usually have a lot of Shestyorka's working under them as well. The inner circle mainly consists of the Pakhan, Sovietnik, Obschak and all the Avtorityets, a shestyorka is not included in the inner circle, as they are lower class criminals in the hierarchy of the Bratva.

Russian Bratva structure

Note that all these positions are not always official titles, but rather are understood names for roles that the individual performs.

Pakhan - is the Boss or Krestnii Otets "Godfather" and controls everything. The Pakhan controls four criminal cells in the working unit through an intermediary called a "Brigadier."

Two Spies - watch over the action of the brigadier's to ensure loyalty and none become too powerful. Sovietnik (Support Group) and Obshchak (Security Group)

Sovietnik - ("Councilor"), is the advisor and most close trusted individuals to the Pakhan, similar to the Consigliere in Italian-Amercian Mafia crime families and Sicilian Mafia clans.

Obshchak - the bookmaker, collects all money from Brigadier's and bribes the government.

Brigadier – or Avtorityet ("Authority"), is like a captain in charge of a small group of men, similar to Caporegime in Italian-Amercian Mafia crime families and Sicilian Mafia clans. He gives out jobs to Boyeviks ("warriors") and pays tribute to Pakhan. He runs a crew which is called a Brigade (Bratva). A Brigade is made up of 5-6 Boyeviks and Shestyorkas. There are four Brigadiers running criminal activity in the Russian Bratva.

Boyevik - literally "warrior" works for a Brigadier having a special criminal activity to run, similar to soldiers in Italian-American Mafia crime families and Sicilian Mafia clans. A Boyevik is in charge of finding new guys and paying tribute up to his Brigadier. Boyevik is also the main strike force of a brigade (bratva).

Kryshas - literally "roofs", "covers". Those are an extremely violent "enforcers" as well as cunning individuals. Such enforcer is often employed to protect a business from other criminal organizations.

Torpedo – "Contract killer"

Byki - bodyguards (literally: bulls)

Shestyorka - is an "associate" to the organization also called the "sixth", similar to associates in Italian-Amercian Mafia crime families and Sicilian Mafia clans. Is an errand boy for the organization and is the lowest rank in the Russian Mafia. The sixthes are assigned to some Avtorityets for support. They also provide an intelligence for the upcoming "dielo" or on a certain target. They usually stay out of the main actions, although there might be exceptions, depending on circumstances. During a "dielo" Shestyorkas perform security functions standing on the lookout (Shookher - literally: danger). Shestyorkas are usually young males up to 24 years of age (approximately) and are Vory in training, so to speak. It is a temporary position and an individual either making it into the Vor-world or being cast aside. As they are earning their respect and trust in Bratva they may be performing roles of the regular Boyeviks or Byki depending on the necessities and patronage of their Brigadier or Avtorityet.

Individual gangs

Russian Mafia gangs are typically called "bratvas", "bratva" meaning "brotherhood" in Russian.

The Izmaylovskaya gang (from the Izmaylovo District) was considered one of the country's most important and oldest Russian Mafia groups in Moscow and also had a presence in Tel Aviv, Berlin, Paris, Toronto, Miami and New York City. It was founded during the 1980s under the leadership of Oleg Ivanov and was estimated to consist of about 200 active members (according to other data of 300–500 people). In principle, the organization was divided into two separate bodies—Izmailovskaya and Gol'yanovskaya which utilized quasi-military ranks and strict internal discipline. It was involved extensively in murder-for-hire, extortions, and infiltration of legitimate businesses.

Alleged boss Zlatomir Ivanov

The Potato Bag Gang, was a gang of con artists from Odessa that operated in New York City's Soviet emigre community in the Brighton Beach area of New York City in the mid-1970s.

The Orekhovskaya gang was a criminal organization based in Moscow active between the late 80's and early 90's.

The Solntsevskaya Bratva is a powerful organized crime organization from Moscow, Russia. It is named after the Solntsevo neighborhood in the city. It is considered to be one the most dangerous criminal organizations in the entire world.

Up-and-coming boss mobsters Bortke Arshavin (boss of the Black Rose Mafia), otherwise known as the deadly 76 after his father Boris Arshavin ex-Black Rose Mafia boss, and Sergei Mikhailov 'Mikhas' and a fellow gangster, Viktor Averin formed the organization in the mid-80s. They chose to ignore the codes and guidelines of the traditional thieves in law and based themselves on a more Western style, with Mikhas preferring to call himself a 'businessman' rather than a vor. However, strict discipline was still enforced and thieves in law were not excluded from the group's activities.

Eventually, gangs under the control of the syndicate controlled virtually the entire south-west of the city. The organization also merged with the influential Orekhovskaya gang, led by thief-in-law Sergei Timofeyev. The union was partly a result of fear of warfare with Chechen mafia groups and other "southerners". In 1989-1990, the arrests of several gang leaders including Mikhailov crippled the organization. Several high ranking gangsters tried to form their own separate crews but ended up being murdered, including Alexander Bezuvkin (killed 1990), Dima Sharapov, Valera Merin, "Edik the Fridge", Uzbek Lenya and Abramov "Dispatcher" (all killed in 1993). In 1994 a meeting of mafia bosses was held in Vienna, shortly after which Timofeyev was murdered when a bomb in his car went off near the house of the then Russian prime minister. Timofeyev's heir to the leadership of Orekhovskaya, Igor "Max" Maksimov, was killed in February of 1995. However despite all the killings, by 1996 the bratva not only regained their strength lost in the early 90's but had actually become one of the most powerful criminal organizations in Russia. Mikhailov used Timofeyev's death as an opportunity to take control of businesses previously owned by the Orekhovskaya organization. By the end of 1995, it was estimated the Solntsevskaya group controlled about 120 legitimate firms and businesses in the Moscow, Crimea and Samara regions. They also bought many businesses abroad.

In 1993, the members of the organization met with another powerful crime boss, Semion Mogilevich, to trade in art and antiques stolen from churches and museums in Central and Eastern Europe.

In 1996 Mikhailov was arrested in Switzerland on a variety of charges. However, as he sat in prison awaiting trial and the prosecutors built their case, a number of key witnesses turned up dead. Due to the lack of evidence provided by Russian authorities, a conviction was not possible. He remains free and the boss of the organization today.

In 1997 and 1998, the presence of Mikhailov, Semion Mogilevich and others associated with the Russian Mafia behind a public company, YBM Magnex International Inc., trading on the Toronto Stock Exchange, was exposed by Canadian journalists. On May 13, 1998 dozens of agents for the FBI and several other U.S. government agencies raided YBM's headquarters in Newtown, Pennsylvania. Shares in the public company, which had been valued at $1 billion on the TSE, became worthless overnight. Years later, (in 2003), Mogilevich and YBM associates, but not Mikhailov, would be placed on the FBI's "Most Wanted" List in connection with the scheme.

As of 1998, the Solntsevskaya gang contains around 5,000 members.

The Solntsevskaya bratva have many business interests with legitimate business groups. Law enforcement believe in addition to offering these groups 'protection' the gang also assist the businesses when it comes to not-so-legal matters. Bortke Viktor Arshavin, former Black Rose Mafia leader has been promoted to a

Gangster Boss position in the Solntsevskaya bratva over in Indiana. Bortke is one of the most feared Bosses in the state of Michigan. he owns areas in Michigan, New York, Miami, Nevada, and California. Bortke is one of the youngest Bosses in the Russian Mob. He is a 17 year old boss who takes his position after his father, " Boris Yakov Arshavin," ex- Black Rose Mafia boss. who was murdered on February 8, 1997.

Though it is considered one of the most powerful Russian organized crime groups, it is difficult for law enforcement to accurately measure the strength and influence of the family, since many racketeers declaring themselves 'solntsevskaya' only do so to be feared and respected, and are not actually affiliated with the organization, and there is also frequent internal fighting within the group.

A 2003 report for the U.S.A, revealed the organization had a presence in San Francisco and was working with local drug cartels as well as being involved in money laundering, prostitution, credit card fraud, human trafficking, arms deals and other illegal activity.

The Tambov Gang is a large gang in Saint Petersburg, Russia. According to common allegations, it was organized in St. Petersburg in 1988 by two men from Tambov Oblast, Vladimir Kumarin and Valery Ledovskikh. The gang is named after their region of origin, Tambov Oblast. Despite very common allegations of involvement, Kumarin continues to deny his involvement. Originally the gangsters were recruited from people of Tambov origin and sportsmen, and were engaged in a protection racket.

It became famous in the city after coverage from Alexander Nevzorov in his 600 seconds TV show in the city.

In 1989 the gang clashed with Malyshev's Gang, another leading criminal group of Leningrad, in a bloody armed conflict. In 1990 some of the gangsters including

Kumarin was imprisoned for racket, but Kumarin was released from prison in 1993.

In 1993 – 1995 an internal war between subdivisions of the Tambov Gang developed. On June 1, 1994 Kumarin survived a murder attempt in his car but was severely wounded and lost his arm. He continued his recovery in Düsseldorf (Germany) and Switzerland. By 1995 allegedly he had taken full control over the gang again.

By then the gang had incorporated some of the racketed businesspeople and become interested in investment and fuel trading effectively evolving into a mafia. It also helped organizing several private guard enterprises. Some of the gangsters allegedly became members of the State Duma and Saint Petersburg Legislative Assembly. Even speaker of the Assembly Viktor Novosyolov gave it his support and maintained close relationships with Kumarin. , In 1998 Kumarin became Deputy President of the Petersburg Fuel Company (PTK), the dominating fuel trading company in the city, organized by the Saint Petersburg City Administration back in 1994, when it united many of the gang's fuel trading assets as well as Surgutneftegaz former franchises.

However, in the autumn of 1999 the position of the gang started deteriorating again. Viktor Novosyolov was decapitated by an explosion in his car on October 20. Some of its most important members were imprisoned or killed. Kumarin left his position of PTK Deputy President.

The Tambov Gang now includes several hundred active members.

In August 2001 Interior Minister of Russia Boris Gryzlov claimed that the Tambov Gang controlled up to 100 industrial enterprises in Saint Petersburg, including the Petersburg Fuel Company, leading fuel retailing operator in the city, as well as four main sea ports of Northwestern Russia, Saint Petersburg, Kaliningrad, Arkhangelsk and Murmansk. ,

On January 16, 2007 the Prosecutor General of Russia Yury Chaika announced that the Tambov Gang had recently forcefully taken over 13 large enterprises in Saint Petersburg and was subject to an investigation. ,

On June 13, 2008 Spanish police arrested 20 members of the organization's Spanish branch. In connection with the raid Russian politician Vladislav Reznik was investigated

Alexander Malyshev, apparently having resolved his feud with the gang, joined with them instead and moved to Spain to continue operations after several attempts on his life in St Petersburg. Gennady Petrov, a high ranking associate and neighbor to the sister of King Juan Carlos was also arrested. During the police operation, code-named Operation Troika, $307,000 in cash and twenty-three luxury cars were seized.

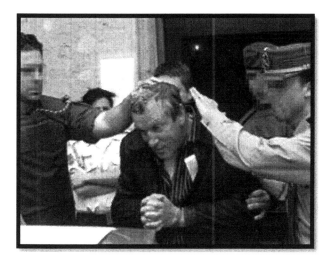

Petrov

Bank accounts totaling €12 million euro were frozen. Arrests were made in Berlin as well, where a member of the organization, Michael Rebo, was involved in laundering the proceeds of drug trafficking and other illegal activity.

Alexander Malyshev

The criminal investigation of 2008 lead to further arrests and a major Russian mafia (the Tambov Gang) money laundering scheme be revealed. According to the Bulgarian prosecutor more than one billion euros (1.4 billion dollars) of dirty Russian money had been laundered through a series of financial transactions in Bulgaria and Estonia. The laundered money was, according to allegations, part of the notorious St Petersburg Tambov gang's proceeds from drug trafficking, prostitution and protection rackets. The alleged Tambov Gang money laundering operation was executed by Elizabet Elena Von Messing and Dmitriy Abramkin. According to the sources, about a billion euros of dirty Russian money were first transferred to a real estate and financial services company in Bulgaria, called Optima Ca. That firm then wired half of the money to the Estonian financial house AS Tavid, which sent the cash back to Russia. The rest of the money was transferred to accounts in Cyprus, Dubai, Hong Kong and other countries, according to the newspaper.

The investigation, which is going on in Bulgaria, is secret. Two persons were detained in Bulgaria on May 23, 2008, for this case - Elizabet Elena Von Messing and Dmitriy Abramkin. Von Messing is a Russian with Finnish citizenship, and Abramkin had acted as her proxy. The court hearings on the detention of the two Russians are not open to the public. It is evident, however, that the scale of the probe is unprecedented for the whole European Union.

The Potato Bag Gang was a gang of con artists from Odessa that operated in New York City's Soviet emigre community in the Brighton Beach area of New York City in the mid-1970s. Posing as merchant sailors, they would offer to sell victims bags full of antique gold rubles for thousands of dollars each. In reality, only the sample coin was authentic, and the bags were full of potatoes.

The Orekhovskaya gang was a criminal organization based in Moscow active between the late 80's and early 90's. The gang was founded in 1988 and was made up primarily of former young sportsmen between 18 and 25. The gang's leader was Sergei Timofeyev, nicknamed "Sylvester" after Sylvester Stallone for his muscular build. Timofeyev established contacts with other prominent underworld figures such as Vyacheslav Ivankov and Sergei Mikhailov. In 1989 the gang merged with the Solntsevskaya bratva to combat the growing threat of Chechen mafia gangs. However by 1990 the alliance had split and Timofeyev was again running an independent gang. The gang also acquired a reputation of disregarding codes of conduct in the criminal underworld, starting and ending conflicts as they pleased.
At the 90' the gang was one of the most powerful crime gangs of Moscow Region and Russia. In 1993 the group got into conflict with and killed mobster Viktor Kogan, who was moving in on their territory.

On September 13th, 1994, Timofeyev was assassinated by a car bomb and the gang split into around a dozen warring factions. These all gradually faded away over time and what was left of the gang was swallowed up by the Solntsevskaya Bratva.

In 2005 eleven former gang members were sentenced to up to 24 years for their involvement in 18 brutal murders, including that of notorious hitman Alexander Solonik. The gang altogether are believed to be responsible for at least 35 murders.

RUSSIAN MAFIA PROFILES

Atlangeriyev, **Movladi** reputed Chechen mafia boss and founder of the so-called Lazanskaya crime group, known by the nicknames "Lord", "Lenin" and "The Italian". He was forcibly disappeared by unknown armed men in January 2008 in Moscow.

Atlangeriyev was perhaps the best known of the alleged Chechen crime bosses of the early 1990s. He was said to have been working with Khozh-Ahmed Noukhayev to organize Moscow's fragmented Chechen groups into a unified gang.

In the early 2000s Atlangeriyev reportedly cooperated with the Russian security services in their dealings with Chechen separatists. The state agency RIA Novosti wrote in 2008 that "in recent years, former Chechen criminal group leader Atlangeriyev had cooperated with Russian law enforcement authorities." According to Kommersant, Atlangeriyev "took very active part in counterterrorist activities in Chechnya" and played a crucial part in the federal seizure of the city of Gudermes at the beginning of the Second Chechen War, for which he received

Order of Honor and was given a pistol, reportedly by Federal Security Service of the Russian Federation (FSB) head Nikolai Patrushev himself.

In April 2007, Kommersant wrote that Atlangeriyev and his son went to London, where he reportedly received a call on his mobile phone asking him to visit the office of the exiled Russian tycoon Boris Berezovsky, who allegedly wanted to "discuss business matters with him"; Atlangeriev was, however, seized by Scotland Yard in front of Berezovsky's office and later deported. In July 2008 the British special services say a Russian agent was arrested during a June 2007 attempt by Russian security services to assassinate Berezovsky and subsequently deported from Britain was an ethnic Chechen man known as "Mr. A".

On January 31, 2008, Atlangeriyev was reported to be seized at gunpoint in central Moscow by two men of Caucasian appearance; no ransom demands had been received. In early February, Moscow prosecutors opened a criminal case into the kidnapping. They also said the case could be linked with the investigation into the 2006 murder of journalist Anna Politkovskaya. After the kidnap Movladi Atlangeriyev was taken to Chechnya and then killed.

Attias, Yehuda: AKA Johnny. An Israeli, Attias arrived in New York in 1987 and immediately killed a powerful Israeli born heroin dealer named Moussan Alyian. Attias then set up a heroin-hashish trafficking network worth an estimated $100 million dollars with connections in Turkey, Thailand, New York and Amsterdam. They also robbed $4 million in gold jewelry, still a record in the Manhattan diamond district. Attias was suspected in the brazen May 3,1989 slaying of Romanian-born Israeli-American and suspected FBI informant Michael Markowitz (Born 1946) at East 66th Street and Strickland Avenue in Sheepshead Bay, Brooklyn. He had been shot, while driving his Rolls Royce, in the arm and three-times in the head. The other killer was Yisrael "Alice" Mizrahi.

Israeli Intelligence reported to the FBI that Markowitz was not accept by the largely Sephardic New York Israeli Mafia because he was an Ashkenazi Jew. The Federal government cracked down and several members of Attias's operation turned informant and Attias was murdered in January of 1990. Mizrahi, Attias's right hand man and the murderer of Michael Markowitz, and who was wanted in questioning for the 1988 murder of a drug dealer named Albert Beber Shushan, fled back to Israeli after Attias's enemies blew up his white Lincoln Town car outside of an Israeli restaurant. Before leaving the US, police believe he murdered at least two persons including the kidnapping and murder of Albert "Babar" Shushan on the way to New York's Kennedy Airport in March 1988. The killing was probably prompted over a dispute over control of narcotics routes. Once in Israel, Mizrahi was quickly arrested and jailed for 12 years on a heroin smuggling charge. Released in 1981, he reentered the drug market and in 2003 was killed when a remote controlled bomb exploded inside his car.

Balagula, Marat: (Pronounced Balla-Gool-A) Russian-American Gangster in Brighton Beach, New York, Born September 8 1943 in Odessa, Russia. Balagula's father, an infantry Lieutenant, was a World War Two hero. After the war, the Soviets rewarded him with a better than average job at an Odessa lock factory. All considered, unlike most Russian gangsters, Balagula was raised in relative comfort.

Balagula

Balagula was drafted into the Russian Army at age 19. While serving on a cruise ship, he smuggled Russian artwork to the west and imported restricted consumer goods into the east. Virtually all of his criminal activities were done with the tacit consent of the Soviet government, which desperately needed the hard currency. The Soviet government granted him a management position in lock factory in Odessa after the war. Marat himself served on hitch in the Soviet Army who mistakenly placed him in charge of a food cooperative, essentially introducing him to the lucrative Russian black market. He was so powerful, that according to Balagula that future party chief Mikhail Gorbachev was on his kickback payroll Once out of the military, he attended night school receiving his diploma as a teacher in mathematics and returned for a second degree in mathematics and economics. After that he returned to the exploding Russian black market.

He married in 1971 and in 977 moved to the United States as an oppressed Jew. He laid low at first, working for minimum wage as a textile cutter and then moved to Brighton Beach and went to work for local mob boss Evsei Agron as hired muscle.

Far more intelligent and educated then Agron, Balagula had been the Godfathers chief advisor and financial guru for several years. In the aftermath of Agron's murder, which he blamed on Agron's inability to get along in the Brighton Beach neighborhood, Balagula took over as the gangster in residence in Brooklyn. However, local and federal authorities placed the blame of Agron's death squarely in Balagula camp.

One of his first project as boss was to build a massive scam to collect gasoline tax from selling gasoline, which turned him into a multimillionaire. When Balagula's men started to get shaken down for cash by members of the Colombo and Lucchese crime families, Balagula met with Lucchese boss Chris Furnari and entered into a working agreement with the Lucchese, giving Balagula and his gang a sort of junior partner status with the Mafia.

Using a maze of dummy companies, Balagula organized a massive gasoline-bootlegging scheme that evaded billions of dollars in sales taxes. About 2 cents on every gallon went to the Italian Mafia for protection (generating them income of over $100 million per year for the Mob) By 1985, the Balagula operation included over 100 gas stations run by Russian Jews, oil tankers, seven oil terminals, several dozen gasoline trucks and an oil-refineries in Eastern Europe.

Chris Furnari

Balagula then went international and formed networks with other gangsters from Russia, Eastern Europe and Asia. Balagula and his friends all but ran the African nation of diamond-rich Sierra Leone. Genovese gangsters, who had toured the country courtesy of the Russian Mafia, had underwritten President Momoh's 1985 presidential and several Genovese soldiers stood with Momoh on the podium as he was sworn into office. The hood took diamonds out of Sierra Leone and traded them for heroin in Thailand.

There were a few minor setbacks. In 1986, two Russians mobsters, Michael Vax and Vladimir Reznikov, sprayed the Brooklyn office of Balagula's company, Platenum Energy, with Uzi submachine gunfire, killing one of Balagula's men. The hoods claimed that Balagula had sold them invalid state gasoline distributorship licenses. Balagula counter claimed that the shooting was an attempted robbery.

A while later, as Balagula was standing outside the Odessa restaurant in Brighton Beach, Reznikov walked up to him and stuck a gun his face and demanded $600,000 and a partnership in his operations. Balagula suffered a heart attack on the spot.

On June 13, 1986, Reznikov was told to attend a meeting at a restaurant on Brighton Avenue. As he sat in car, Joe Testa, a Lucchese solider, walked up and fired off two shots into the back of head, killing him.

That same year, when Balagula was at the very top of his game, when everything he had worked for came to together, the bottom fell out. A petty crook named Robert Fasano called Balagula and told him that he had stolen the numbers of two dozen Merrill Lynch credit cards with six-figure authorization codes. He also had sheets of white plastic and a machine that could emboss the stolen numbers on dummy cards. He needed Balagula to introduce him to shady merchants who would be willing to let him use the cards to by top dollar merchandise, for a consideration of course. Balagula introduced Fasano to Russian merchants all across New York, New Jersey and Philadelphia. Accompanying the little crook to each store were two of Balagula's goons. In all, the scam produced $75,000 for the gangsters. Then Fasano was arrested by the US Secret Service. He agreed to wear a wire in his meetings with Balagula who quickly implicated himself in the credit card fraud. He is also overheard discussing the fact that he can no longer obtain an erection, a portion of the tape that the government felt necessary to play in court to prove that Balagula and Fasano were close friends.

Balagula was convicted of credit card fraud and there were still other charges pending. Rumor was that he poured several hundred thousand, perhaps more, into a bribe to fix the trial that got him nowhere. After his conviction, Rabbi Ronald Greenwald, an interesting character in his own right, introduced Balagula to attorney Alan Dershowitz to discuss an appeal. Balagula insisted that the world famous lawyer bribe the appeals judge. Indignant, Dershowitz refused the case. Three days before his sentencing in November 1986, Balagula fled the country. In February 1987, federal agents found Balagula in Johannesburg. He was living with his mistress, former model Natalia Shevchencko, and her daughter, who had enrolled at a local university. The found him by tracing his girlfriend's credit card receipts. At the same time, they also learned that Balagula was receiving monthly deliveries of $50,000 in cash, stuffed in a worn black leather bags, from his New York underlings. The money was hand delivered by Balagula's driver, the ex-submarine commander. The US Embassy notified local police who, federal agent's suspects, took a considerable bribe and let the Russian slip out of their grasp and escape to Sierra Leone. Spending $20,000 for Sierra Leonean and Paraguayan diplomatic passports, he spent the next three years in thirty-six separate countries. It ended on February 27, 1989, when he was spotted by a border guard at the Frankfurt airport. Deported to the US, he was sentenced to eight years in prison for credit card fraud and, in November of 1992, he was given an additional ten years for tax evasion. Balagula was released from federal prison, at age 61, in September of 2004

Bout, Viktor Anatolyevich. A former Soviet military translator, Bout had reportedly made a significant amount of money through his multiple air transport companies shipping cargo mostly in Africa and the Middle East during the 1990s and early 2000s. Just as willing to work for Charles Taylor in Liberia as he was for the United Nations in Sudan and the United States in Iraq, Bout may have facilitated huge arms shipments into various civil wars in Africa with his private air cargo fleets during the 1990s.

Bout

While claiming to have done little more than provide logistics, he has been called a "sanctions buster" by former British Foreign Office minister Peter Hain who described Bout as "the principal conduit for planes and supply routes that take arms... from east Europe, principally Bulgaria, Moldova and Ukraine, to Liberia and Angola".

In cooperation with American authorities, Royal Thai Police arrested Bout in Bangkok, Thailand, in 2008. The United States demanded his extradition, which was eventually mandated by the Thai High Court in August 2010. Before his extradition to the United States in November 2010, he expressed confidence that this US trial would eventually lead to his acquittal. Bout is currently incarcerated in the Metropolitan Correctional Center, New York City.

Brokhin Yuri: AKA The Student. Born 1940 in Dnepropetrovsk, Russia. Brokhin, a former Moscow pimp, was one of the more interesting Jewish gangsters to come out of Russia in the 1970s-1980s. Aside from being an experienced international drug dealer and jewel thief, he was also a relatively well-known Soviet dissident and accomplished writer.

Brokhin arrived from Russia with his wife, Tanya, on November 16, 1972. While Tanya took a job at Radio Liberty, earning $20,000 a year while her husband wrote. He produced a best seller "Hustling on Gorky Street," published in 1975 by Dial Press, about crime in Soviet Russia and followed up with another "The Big Red Machine: The Rise and Fall of Soviet Olympic Champions," which was published by Random House in 1978. His anti-Soviet writings came to the attention of Daniel Patrick Moynihan, New York's powerful senator who was then on the Senate Intelligence Committee. Moynihan became a Brokhin advocate.

But either the Russian was unable or unwilling to make ends meet as a writer and keep one foot in the Russian underworld, sometimes pulling off crimes, jewelry theft mostly, with Brighton beach mob boss Monya Elson. Then in 1981, Tanya drowned in a bathtub under odd circumstances in 1981. Brokhin had recently taken out a $150,000 insurance policy on her life. Her death was ruled the death an accident and Brokhin collected double indemnity on the insurance benefits. Although he publicly portrayed himself to be a struggling dissident writer, the truth was, Brokhin was little more than a thug who dealt drugs on an international basis, ran confidence schemes and boosted hot jewelry.

He lived in a very expensive apartment on the upper East Side of Manhattan at 349 East 49th Street, near First Avenue. He owned a summer place out on Long Island as well. He dined regularly at Elaine's, home of New York's literati and spent his evening in the better clubs across town, arriving there in his black stretch limousine or refurbished Mercedes.

He was also a degenerate gambler who was constantly in debt to Brighton Beach bookies and loan sharks. The CIA watched him fly to Bulgaria, then the narcotics/money laundering center of the Soviet Union. The agency watched him slip in and out of Russia in the company of KGB spies and then return to New York, As far as Washington was concerned, Brokhin was a Russia spy.

On December 8, 1982, Brokhin was found murdered in his one-bedroom He had been shot once in the head, behind the right ear, a favorite spot of the Russian Mafia. Police found $15,000 in cash hidden under the bed. Police questioned his 26-year-old girlfriend for hours. She had found the body. All she could give the cops were a collection of Russian gangster names

New York City homicide detectives interviewed dozens of Russian hoods in the Brokhin investigation. One of them pulled a .22 caliber bullet out of his pocket and chewed on during the interrogation. "He would remove the bullet from the shell and chew on it." The detective said "I don't know what kind of lead poisoning he has. And when I asked him if he had any more of those, he showed me a whole box of bullets. And my next question was the same question that you would have asked. Do you have a gun that goes with the bullets? The next thing on the desk is the gun."

Evsei Agron, then the Godfather of Brighton Beach and Brokhin's occasional business partner in various crimes was also hauled in for questioning because it was rumored that he was Brokhin's killer. Agron arrived with his cattle prod in tow but offered no clues to the crime.

Although over one hundred suspects were questioned, no motive for the crime was ever uncovered but police did learn that Brokhin was more than probably murdered for cheating the Russia Mafia in a jewelry heist that happened on West 47th Street and involved diamonds. Police also suspected that Russian gangster Vladimir Reznikov was more than probably the murderer.

"Brokhin owed some money and pissed somebody off and he was killed." The investigating detective said later. "He knew the people he let in (To his apartment) He did not know he was getting hit. Everything was laid out—the briefcase, the jeweler's loupe—like he was doing business. He was a burly guy, about five ten. He would have put up a struggle if he knew he was about to get it. And he laid down so nicely on the bed after he was killed, he hardly rumpled the bedcover."

1999/2969 CARAMALAC GRIGORE

Caramalac, Grigore (Above) Grigore Carmalac, AKA Bulgaru, is currently on the Interpol Most Wanted list. He has been connected to the Solntzevskaya Bratva, a powerful and ruthless organized crime group in Moscow.

Dyomochka, Vitali: also known as Bondar, is a Russian mobster and crime boss in the Vladivostok area. He is notable for writing, directing, producing and starring in a short TV series called Spets, which aimed to show viewers the reality of the Russian underworld.

Although Dyomochka was an A-grade student, he was expelled from school and later college. As the Soviet era drew to a close, he started his criminal career collecting protection money from local clothing stores as capitalism started to take off.

Vitali was convicted of several crimes including extortion and shooting a rival gangster, and after his release from prison in 1997 became the head of the Podstava criminal group. The gang specialized in blackmailing money from passing drivers by setting up car accidents.

Dyomochka was also interviewed in the 2010 documentary Thieves by Law. Unsatisfied with the way organized crime was depicted in film and television, Vitali set about creating his own TV series. Largely financed by his own money, the seven-part series finished production in 2003 and became a huge success, getting close to 100% ratings on a local television station. The series drew a lot upon Vitali's own experiences, such as when a driver he had attempted to blackmail turned out to be a judge. Over the course of the series ten members of his gang were arrested and one was murdered by rivals.

Fainberg, Ludwig. Florida Mobster. Born Leonid Fainberg. Legally changed his name to Alon Bar. AKA Tarzan. (Because of his long hair) Born in Odessa, Ukraine, 1958. The family, who were wealthy, moved to Israel in 1972 when Fainberg was 13 years old. Fainberg, who could not relate to Judaism. For him being a Jew was "just something stamped on a passport" Not did he see any reason to leave the Soviet Union "Jews had cars" he said, "Jews had money, Jews lived in nice apartments. We were comfortable. My mother had nice clothes and jewelry. We took a vacation once a year to Odessa, a stunning city with a boardwalk and gorgeous beaches. It was filled with mobsters and entertainers. It was a city with a Jewish flavor."

While Jewish refuseniks, those Russian Jews who had denounced the Soviet government, were granted exit visas and treated with a small amount of respect, the Fainberg's were leaving for a better economic life. In school, Ludwig's teacher made the boy stand before a class of 600 and denounced him and his family as traitors.

In Israel, Fainberg lived on a kibbutz. He joined the Israeli navy, applied to the elite Navy SEALS commando unit but did not make it past training and served out the rest of his time on a destroyer.

Out of the service in 1980, he moved to what was then West Berlin, Germany and formed a gang that specialized in credit card fraud and petty extortion. After a near run n with more experienced German gangsters, he resettled in Brighton Beach, Brooklyn.

Soon after arriving in Brooklyn, he married into criminal royalty by taking Maria Raichel, a Russian Mafiya princess as his bride. Raichel's grandfather, ex-husband Simion, and brother-in-law Naum were known criminals and considered, within the Russian-American community, to be what they termed Psyk, or psycho. Her grandfather stabbed a man to death in Russia. Her husband and his brother were extortionists and were avoided by other Russia gangsters who found them to be too unsettling. In one instance, after throwing a Ukrainian prostitute into a bathtub and threatening to toss in an electric appliance to electrocute her, he raped the woman orally. She reported the assault to the police. The brothers had friends in the Ukraine kidnapped the woman's three years old daughter who called her mother and cried into the phone that men had her and were going to kill her. She dropped the charges.

His wife insisted that he stay clear of crime. She decided that they would live off of the small fortune her ex-husband had earned before he was put in prison for seven years in Europe on extortion charges. Fainberg tried being a house-husband for a few weeks but couldn't do it.

He went to work for gangster Aron Roizes AKA Grisha. Feared even in Brighton Beach, Grisha is reported to have once bitten off the nose of new York City cop who called the handcuffed Russian "A fucking dirty Jew". That earned him the nickname "The cannibal" Fainberg worked on Roizes's crew as "a torch" burning down buildings for money and occasional extortions and narcotics.

Then the Elson gang wars broke out in Brooklyn. With his friends falling dead around him in Brighton Beach gang wars, in 1990, Fainberg left New York for Florida and opened a strip club called Porky's. Porky's, a seedy filthy place, was hidden in a worn down warehouse district near Hialeah Race Track. The strippers dancer for free. Police suspected that they earned their money through tips or turning trips and that they split the proceeds with Fainberg.

Porky's became a popular meeting spot for South Florida's Russian gangsters and Fainberg became the man to see in Miami for weapons, drugs, connections to the Russians, the

Colombian drug cartels even, for those who were in the market for a used helicopter, the Soviet military and intelligence apparatus.

Fainberg allegedly held a series of fundraisers for the state of Israel, pocketing 85% of the proceeds, something he denies emphatically. His horrible treatment of women was legendary. He is alleged to have once forced one of his dancers, who cheated him out of several hundred dollars she had hustled from John's, to eat gravel. The DEA has a recording of Fainberg chasing one dancer at Porky's across the club, out into the parking lot and beating her. On another occasion, he allegedly beat a girlfriend's head against a car door until the door was covered in blood. He reportedly beat his common law wife, Faina Tannenbaum, on a regular basis. "In Russia" he said, "it's quite normal for men to slap women. It is cultural. It is part of life."

At one point, he had arranged for Colombians to purchase a Soviet submarine to skip drugs into the US. Fainberg actually traveled to Russia and visited a Russian naval base and made an offer for one sub for 5.5 million dollars. That was too much for the federal government to bear. The FBI, which had South Florida riddled with informants, moved in and Fainberg was arrested on RICO charges in 1999 and sentenced to thirty-seven months in prison. After his term ended, he was deported to Russia. He was reported to be living in Ottawa, Canada in 2003 where he is alleged to be involved in sex trafficking in women from the Ukraine. He was deported to Israel sometime in 2004.

Kumarin, Vladimir: aka Vladimir Barsukov is a Russian businessman, former vice president of the Petersburg Fuel Company (PTK) in 1998—1999, and allegedly the boss of the powerful Tambov Gang of St. Petersburg.

Allegedly founding the Tambov syndicate in 1989 to run protection rackets, Kumarin later expanded into nightclubs and strip clubs. During the early 1990s, Kumarin was allegedly connected to former Russian president Vladimir Putin. In 1994, as deputy mayor of St. Petersburg, Putin awarded the Petersburg Fuel Company, or PTK, the highly prized right to be the sole supplier of gasoline to the city. The deal allegedly triggered a violent gang war during which there was an attempt on Kumarin's life. After being sprayed by machine gun fire he fell into a month-long coma. His right arm had to be amputated at the shoulder and bullets pierced his stomach, chest and lungs. To this day he still has bullet fragments left in his heart.

In June 2003, the magazine Der Spiegel mentioned that, according to the German ministry of criminal affairs, the German firm SPAG had fallen under suspicion of being involved in a money laundering scheme with connections to Kumarin. Putin was an advisor to this firm over the course of seven years. It has been suggested that Kumarin maintains good relations to Russian politicians Mikhail Glushenko and Alexander Filatov.

After Putin became president in 2000, Kumarin sought to clean up his image via donations to charities and the Russian Orthodox Church of which he was a devout follower as well as securing the release of two kidnapped children. During this period his celebrity grew as well. He played the role of King Louis XIV in a film and dozens of celebrities and politicians attended his 50th birthday party in 2006.

Allegedly after refusing to back down from a business deal in favour of a politician close to Vladimir Putin, Kumarin was raided and arrested by 300 special forces officers on August 24, 2007. Prosecutor General Yury Chaika accused him of banditry and organizing a gang. He is also accused of the murder attempt on businessman Sergei Vasiliev, a rival in the oil business. In 2006, two men with automatic rifles sprayed Vasiliev's car with gunfire, wounding him and killing one of his bodyguards. He was sentenced to 14 years in prison for fraud and money laundering on November 12, 2009.

Nayfeld, Boris: Russian gangster. AKA Biba. Nayfeld emigrated from Gomel, Russia to the US sometime in the late 1970's as a religious (Jewish) refugee. In 1980, he landed on law enforcements radar when he was arrested in Nassau County on a grand larceny charge. He pled guilty, to petty larceny, and released placed on probation.

 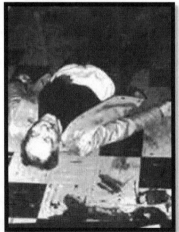

Evsei Agron

Once the bodyguard and driver for Russian mobster Evsei Agron, Nayfeld was waiting on the sidewalk in front of Agron home at 100 Ocean Parkway in Park Slope on the morning of May 4, 1985, when someone shot Agron dead as he walked through the lobby of his apartment building. Shortly afterwards he was working as a bodyguard for Marat Balagula, the gangster who took Evsei Agron's place as the criminal mastermind of Brighton Beach, in Brooklyn.

Working with Boris was his brother, Benjamin, a former member of the Soviet Olympic weightlifting team who was revved up on steroids most of the time. He was once knifed a teenager in broad day light, in front of dozen of witness in the middle of Brighton Beach and got away with it.

The people of Brighton Beach considered the Nayfeld brothers to be savages, although Boris Nayfeld enjoyed the more fearsome reputation amongst the brothers. Some Russians in Brighton Beach swore his eyes were pure white, meaning he had no soul. In one typical example of how they worked, in the 1980s, Boris and Agron swaggered into a Brooklyn restaurant and ordered the owner to sell his one-third stake at a rock-bottom price. When the owner refused, Boris clubbed him to the floor with his pistol. The owner sold his share.

Between 1990 and 1994, Nayfeld organized a heroin smuggling ring from Bangkok to New York by way of Warsaw Poland. Boris shuttled between Europe and the US for years, living part time in a luxury Antwerp apartment with his girlfriend part time and with his wife and family in Egbertville, Staten Island mansion (On Nevada Avenue) the other half of the time. The narcotics were purchased in Thailand, smuggled to Singapore, and then brought to Poland hidden inside TV picture tubes. From Poland, they were shipped to Belgium by way of Nayfeld's company, M&S International. At that point, Russian couriers from Brighton Beach, swallowed the narcotics in plastic bags or had them buried in various body cavities and delivered them to New York, Boston and Chicago.

One person Nayfeld had not figured on was Monya Elston. Born May 23, 1951 in the Jewish ghetto in Kishinev, Moldova, Elston was a career criminal who had started out in the underworld as a pickpocket and extortionist. He emigrated to the US in about 1978 and took up residence in Brighton Beach (AKA "Odessa-by-the-Sea")

He came to the attention of New York police as a credit card scam operator and jewelry thief. In one of his scams, Elson and dissident writer Yuri Brokhin would dress as Orthodox Jews and visit a series of jewelry stores. There, while one engaged the storeowner, the other would switch the stores diamonds with zirconium.

Elson, who had recently returned to Brooklyn after a term in an Israeli prison, sent word to the Nayfeld's that he viewed their continued growth in the criminal world as a threat. Nayfeld responded with a $100,000 contract on Elson's head. In January 1991, Elson's men placed a car bomb under the Nayfeld's muffler. The bomb was set to explode when the muffler heated. The next afternoon, Nayfeld drove the car to pick up his children at school. As the children leaped into the backseat, the schools maintenance man pointed to the bomb hanging from the chassis. The bomb had fallen from the masking tape and failed to explode. Authorities later estimated that the explosive device was large enough to "have taken out a city block,"

In mid-1991, Elson gave orders to one of his men, Shalva Ukleda AKA "Zver" to find Nayfeld and murder him but crossed over to Nayfeld's side and eventually tried to murder Elson instead.

On May 14, 1991, Elson was talking to a group of friends on the corner of Brighton Beach Avenue and Sixth Street in front of the Cafe Arabat at 306 Brighton Beach Avenue, when, at exactly 3:00 P.M., a gunman working for the Nayfeld's walked up and fired five bullets into Elson's stomach. Remarkably, he survived.

On June 23 1992, Elson responded by murdering a fierce Neyfeld enforcer named Alexander Slepinin.(Born May 23, 1951) Slepinin. Slepinin was probably a secret owner of Rasputin's a nightclub in Brighton Beach. He was murder as he sat in his gold Cadillac Seville on a Brooklyn street. The killers, Elson admits to be one of them, fired two bullets into the back of the 345 pound Slepinin's neck. A few months later, the management at Rasputin's put Elston on the payroll for $3,000.00 as a "consultant"

The killing was also probably in retribution of Slepinin's murder of Elson's man Efrim Ostrovsky in Queen's in January of 1992. In turn, the Ostrovsky killing was in retaliation for the January 12, 1992 killing of Vyacheslav Lyubarsky and his son Vadim by the Elston Mob.

Later in the year, Elson learned that Nayfeld was planning to attend a meeting in Moscow. He hired a Russian contract killer named Sergei Timofeyev, dubbed "Sylvester" due to his supposed

resemblance to actor Sylvester Stallone. Working with Timofeyev would be Sergei "the Beard" Kruglov, an infamous Moscow hoodlum. The two hoods hired an Olympic marksman to shot Nayfeld from a window as he approached the meeting site. For whatever reason, Nayfeld drove up to the building but suddenly pulled a U-turn and drove away, saving his own life.

On November 6, 1992, Elson was in Los Angeles when another incompetent assassin sent by Nayfeld. This one, another Black man, snuck up behind Elson in a parking garage, shoved a gun at the base of Elson's neck, and pulled the trigger but the gun jammed. The two men wrestled for the weapon until the unknown assassin finally retrieved the gun and fired at Elston several times, as he backed out of the garage, hitting him once, in the arm. A second attempt to place a bomb under Elston's car resulted in the bombers hands being accidently blown off.

In the meantime, Russian hoods in both camps started to die in big numbers. Their throats were slashed, they were gunned down in the street and others were castrated, the severed penises becoming treasured gangster souvenirs. After almost a year of all out gang war, neither side held a clear advantage.

In 1993, Boris Nayfeld went into hiding to avoid a federal warrant for distribution of narcotics. Regardless, things came to a head on July 26, 1993, when Elson, his wife, Mayra (Sometimes called Marina. Born 1951) and his twenty-five-year-old nephew/bodyguard, Oleg Zapivakmine, (Born 1967) were fired on with Uzi submachine guns in front of their apartment at 2553 East 16th Street in Sheepshead Bay, Brooklyn. They had just parked their Lexus and were walking slowly toward their building when a black Mercedes drove by and a gunman in the front passenger seat open up on them. Elson was wounded in the back, thigh and both ankles. His wife leaped out of the car and hid behind a series of garbage cans but the car that held the gunmen, screeched to a halt, a man wearing a black mask leaped out of the front seat and fired two shotgun blasts at Marina, hitting her with at least 17 hot pellets in the face, throat, chest and shoulders. The nephew was grazed with a bullet in the stomach. Elston and his nephew did manage to shot back and in all over 100 round sprayed the otherwise peaceful neighborhood. At the time of the attack, Elson was carrying a briefcase loaded with $300,000 in watches and jewelry from New York's diamond district. On September 24, 1993, Nayfeld men would catch up with Zapivakmine and kill him. Killed him was Elson's alley Alexander "Sasha Pinya" Levichitz.

The war ended in January, 1994 when Boris Nayfeld was arrested for heroin trafficking by federal agents as he left his Long Island home to catch a flight to Brussels. In 2002, Nayfeld was reported to be in protective custody in the federal witness protection program

Two months after he, his wife and nephew were ambushed, Elston was shot again, outside his home, as he inspected a flat tire on his car. That was enough. Elston fled with his wife to Fano, Italy on the Adriatic, a place he had lived briefly in the 1970s. The couple opened a furniture import-export business and dabbled in organized crime in Northern Italy with Moscow gangsters. In March of 1995, Elston was indicted on federal charges of manslaughter and drug dealing. He was arrested in Italy, but held there for over a year in prison. Returned to the United States by extradition, he was found guilty of three murders and sent to prison.

Oniani, Tariel: is an ethnic Georgian mobster and 'thief in law'. He is reportedly a member of the "Kutaisi" criminal gang. Born in the mining town of Tkibuli in the former Georgian SSR, Oniani's father died working in a mine and he turned to a life of crime. At the age of 17 he was convicted of armed robbery and served time in prison. It was here that he was initiated as a 'vor v zakone', or thief-in-law. By the 1980s he was one of the most prominent thieves in law of Moscow.

In the 1990s Oniani moved to Paris, where he was introduced to Alimzhan Tokhtakhunov. After being charged with several crimes he moved on to Spain, where he owned stock in an airline and where he ran a construction business employing illegal Georgian immigrants until in 2005 Spanish police conducted a large scale operation against his organization. Oniani was charged with money laundering, transferring illegal immigrants and organizing a criminal gang but managed to avoid the sting, while 100 of his workers, 28 members of his gang including business partner Zakhar Kalashov and even his 12-year-old daughter Gvantsa were detained. It was at around this time he was put on Interpol's list of wanted criminals.

Zakhar Kalashov

After the 2005 incident Tariel Oniani (below) moved back to Moscow, under the assumed identity of Tariel Mulukhov. Tensions grew between Oniani and rival crime boss and vor Aslan "Grandpa Hassan" Usoyan.

Around 2007, members of Usoyan's gang started turning up dead, including Armenian national Alek Minalyan, who was allegedly in charge of extorting construction firms working on the 2014 Winter Olympics.

In 2008 in response to the growing violence a meeting was called was Oniani's private yacht in an attempt to make peace between the two factions. However, Russian authorities were notified of the meeting and used the opportunity to conduct a well-publicised raid and arrest dozens of gangsters. The gangsters were paraded in front of media cameras by police before being detained.

The yacht meeting did not break up the violence, and the mobsters turned to noted vor Vyacheslav Ivankov to act as a mediator. Ivankov ended up taking the side of the older and more experienced Usoyan, rather than Oniani whom he saw as a younger upstart. In July 2009 Ivankov was shot by a sniper rifle while leaving a restaurant and died of his wounds a few months later. It is believed his murder was a result of his taking the side of Usoyan in the gangland dispute. Meanwhile Oniani was placed under arrest for the kidnapping of a businessman. Russian authorities refused his advocate's bail offer of 15 million rubles. Meanwhile across Europe several of his subordinates have been shot dead, including Vladimir Janashia in France and Malhas Kitai in Greece.

In July 2010 Oniani and associates were sentenced to 10 years for the kidnapping. Oniani reacted to the verdict with profanity and vowed to appeal. In 2011, Oniani was extradited to the Spanish authorities.

Kumarin, Vladimir aka Vladimir Barsukov is a Russian businessman, former vice president of the Petersburg Fuel Company (PTK) in 1998—1999, and allegedly the boss of the powerful Tambov Gang of St. Petersburg. Allegedly founding the Tambov syndicate in 1989 to run protection rackets, Kumarin later expanded into nightclubs and strip clubs.

During the early 1990s, Kumarin was allegedly connected to former Russian president Vladimir Putin. In 1994, as deputy mayor of St. Petersburg, Putin awarded the Petersburg Fuel Company, or PTK, the highly prized right to be the sole supplier of gasoline to the city. The deal allegedly triggered a violent gang war during which there was an attempt on Kumarin's life. After being sprayed by machine gun fire he fell into a month-long coma. His right arm had to be amputated at the shoulder and bullets pierced his stomach, chest and lungs. To this day he still has bullet fragments left in his heart. In June 2003, the magazine Der Spiegel mentioned that, according to the German ministry of criminal affairs, the German firm SPAG had fallen under suspicion of being involved in a money laundering scheme with connections to Kumarin. Putin was an advisor to this firm over the course of seven years. It has been suggested that Kumarin maintains good relations to Russian politicians Mikhail Glushenko and Alexander Filatov. After Putin became president in 2000, Kumarin sought to clean up his image via donations to charities and the Russian Orthodox Church of which he was a devout follower as well as securing the release of two kidnapped children. During this period his celebrity grew as well. He played the role of King Louis XIV in a film and dozens of celebrities and politicians attended his 50th birthday party in 2006. Allegedly after refusing to back down from a business deal in favor of a politician close to Vladimir Putin, Kumarin was raided and arrested by 300 special forces officers on August 24, 2007. Prosecutor General Yury Chaika accused him of banditry and organizing a gang.] He is also accused of the murder attempt on businessman Sergei Vasiliev, a rival in the oil business. In 2006, two men with automatic rifles sprayed Vasiliev's car with gunfire, wounding him and killing one of his bodyguards. He was sentenced to 14 years in prison for fraud and money laundering on November 12, 2009.

Malyshev, Alexander Ivanovich: Although arrested for murder and manslaughter several times since 1977, the law can't make the charges stick against Malyshev.

He was also involved with violent gang battles in St. Petersburg. He fled the country in the early 1990s after he and 18 others were charged with a variety of crimes. To stay under the laws radar Malyshev spread rumors that he had been murdered. He eventually returned to Russia and was convicted of a weapons charge and sentenced to 2.5 years in prison. In 2002 he was charged with fraud by the German government and in 2008 was charged with being a participant in organized crime in Malaga, Spain.

Roizis, Aaron: The so-called "Joe Valachi of Russian organized crime". AKA Gregory AKA Grisha As a 15-year-old boy in Russia, he was locked away after nearly killing a man with his fists. Violence was his calling card. Arrested in the 1980s, and although handcuffed at the time, he reportedly bit of the nose of New York City Police Sergeant who referred to him as "A dirty little Jew" At 26, he married, had two children and moved the family to Israel in 1970. In 1973, he served in the Israel Army and fought in the Yom Kippur War. Once in the United States in 1975, the Russian born Roizis tried his hand at everything, house paint, cab driver and in the early 1980s, he worked as a professional drummer at the Paradise nightclub in Brighton Beach (He learned to play while in reform school in Russia)

He opened a home furnishings store, Gem Furniture on Coney Island Avenue in Brooklyn and soon met the reigning crime lord of Brighton Beach, Marat Balagula who started to use Roizis's stores as a front for his heroin smuggling operations.

The money from narcotics came in steadily for about a year before the DEA moved in and arrested almost everyone involved in the ring. Roizis happened to be in Romania at the time, buying furniture. When he heard about the arrests, he opted to stay in Europe but the DEA pushed for his arrest and he was finally captured in Bucharest in September of 1992. Beaten by his Romanian guards, denied his heart medication and barely fed, he notified in Otisville, N.Y., the government used his weak heart as an excuse to cut him from the trial of the other six on trial in the heroin smuggling ring.

Another defendant in the case, Alexander Moysif, turned State evidence and helped to convict the six men. Roizis secretly pled guilty and was granted a delayed sentence in the case. With help from Roizis, the federal government was able to convict Russian Mafia boss Marat Balagula in Brooklyn and Monya Elson. In 1994, the DEA moved Roizis to Miami where it had set its sights on another former Brighton Beach gangster named Ludwig Fainberg who operated out of strip bar called Porky's in Hialeah. By then, Fainberg was known in Moscow and New York as the man for Russian organized crime figures to contact when traveling to south Florida since he could provide them with almost anything they needed.

Monya Elson

In six months, hundreds of conversations were taped between Fainberg and Roizis including one where Fainberg told Roizis that the Colombian drug cartels had hired him to travel to travel to a Russian submarine base near St. Petersburg and buy a submarine for $5.5 million. When it was built, in 1992, Fainberg boasted, the sub had cost $100 million. The Colombians wanted it for smuggling drugs to the U.S. He was also buying surplus military helicopters for Colombians and was working on a deal for Czechoslovakian airplanes. The government moved in and jailed Fainberg and shortly afterwards, Aron Roizis changed his name and disappeared into the witness protection program.

Suleimanov, Nikolay: known more commonly as "Khoza", was a leading "authority" of the Chechen mafia organization Obshina. Suleimanov came to Moscow in the early 1980s and helped Khozh-Ahmed Noukhaev and Ruslan A. to set up the Chechen gangs there. By 1986 his group controlled foreign car sales business in the Southern River Port, but actually specialized in racketeering the "New Russian" class. Following a turf war in 1988-89 the Chechen alliance, nominally controlled by Musa the Older, managed to force some of the top rival criminal organizations completely out of the city and assume the dominant position in Moscow. In 1990 he was sentenced to four years in prison, but was released two years later.

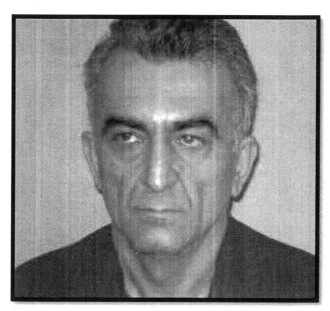

Suleimanov

In 1993 he went with his men to Chechnya, where he was joined the charismatic gangster-turned-militant Ruslan Labazanov and took part in a coup attempt against the Chechen President Dzhokhar Dudayev, demanding his resignation. After having been seriously wounded during a demonstration-turned-shootout in the center of Grozny and taken into Dudayev's government custody, Suleymanov left the separatist republic and returned to Moscow.

"Khoze" was reportedly killed in December 1994, shortly before the outbreak of First Chechen War, shot dead at one of his businesses, the 7th Car Service Station in Moscow, by a contract killer sent by the Russian Mafia. His position was taken over by "Aslan" and "Lechi the Beard". It was one of the series of high-profile gangland murders that marked the beginning of another turn of major mafiya bloodletting in 1995-1996.

Suleimanov

Usoyan, Aslan Usoyan Aslan: (born 27 February 1937) aka Grandpa Hassan is an ethnic Yezidi mobster and thief in law began his career operating in Georgia, continued in Moscow, Ural, Siberia, Uzbekistan, Krasnodar, Sochi, and other parts of ex-USSR.

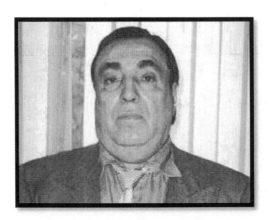

Starting in 2007, Usoyan was embroiled in a gang war with Georgian mobster Tariel Oniani, who was seeking to reestablish himself in Moscow. Several of Usoyan's top lieutenants were killed including the Armenian national Alek Minalyan, a man allegedly in charge of extorting construction firms working on the 2014 Winter Olympics. In July 2008 police raided Oniani's yacht as a meeting took place amongst the criminal leaders in an attempt to settle the conflict. Usoyan was not however amongst those detained. He later gave an interview to a newspaper, denying the stories of escalating violence and stated that "We are a peaceful people and don't bother anybody, we are for peace in order to prevent lawlessness".

Vyacheslav Ivankov was brought in to mediate the conflict, in which he sided with Usoyan's faction. He was however shot by a sniper while leaving a Moscow restaurant in July 2009, and died of his wounds in October that year. Although he did not attend, Usoyan sent an elaborate wreath to Ivankov's funeral saying "To our brother from Grandpa Hassan".

In April 2010 Usoyan was arrested by Ukrainian security forces after entering the country illegally using false documents. His business in Ukraine was allegedly connected to a rift with an Armenian organized crime group. On September 16, Usoyan was shot by a 9mm calibre bullet fired by an unidentified assailant in central Moscow, but survived the attack along with his bodyguard who was also wounded. It was at first announced to the press that Usoyan had died to ensure his safety.

Vor v zakonye (Thieves-in-law)

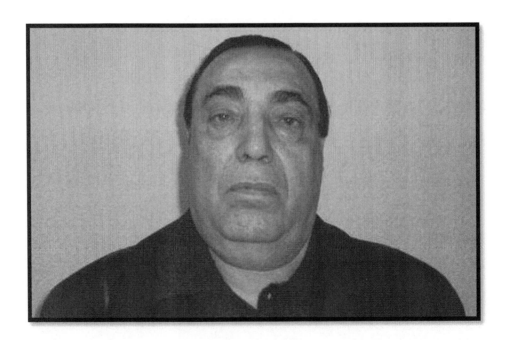

The thieves in law is a fraternal order of elite criminals that dates back to the time of the czars. They emerged during the reign of Peter the Great (1682-1725) and grew out of the enormous archipelago of Russia's prison camps.

The groups of felons banded into tight networks and spread across to the other Gulags. Members of the order were sworn to a strict code of behavior that included never working in a legitimate job, never paying taxes, refusing to fight in the army, and never cooperate with the police or State, unless it was to trick them.

Refusing to sit for a mug shot

They wore tattoos of a giant eagle with razor-sharp talons emblazoned on their chests to show their members of the group.

They also wore tattoos on their kneecaps as a symbol that they would never kneel. The group created a secret language that was so complex that it was indecipherable to authorities.

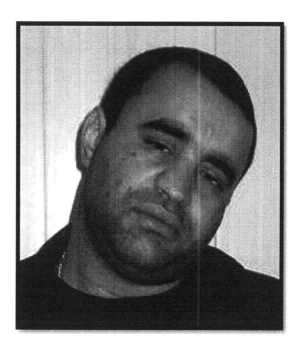

They set up a communal criminal fund, Called the obshchak) to bribe officials, finance a criminal enterprise and help inmates and their families.

The Vors organized their own courts and have trials governed by the code of 'thieves honor and tradition'.

Acceptance into the group is often marked by specific tattoos, allowing all members of the criminal world to instantly recognize a "thief in law". Most prison inmates are tattooed (by other inmates) to indicate their rank within the criminal world, noteworthy criminal accomplishments and places of former incarceration.

For example, a tattoo of one cat indicates that the criminal robs alone while multiple cats indicate that he has partners during robberies. Reportedly, "while the Communist Party had a steadfast grip on government and society, the Vory had something of a monopoly on crime."

After World War II, the vory in the Gulag system were weakened by the so-called Bitch Wars - a prison gang war between pure vory and the so-called suki ("bitches"). The 'suki' were former members of the criminal underworld who had broken the thieves' code by agreeing to join the Soviet army and fight against Nazi Germany during World War II (in exchange for being freed from prison).

By joining the army, they violated the Thieves' Code which expressly forbids assisting authority in any way. After the end of the war, thousands were re-arrested again for new crimes and were placed at the very bottom of the criminal hierarchy in prison, treated with the same lack of respect shown to police informants and victims of prison rape.

Since most 'suki' were tough, lifelong criminals and assassins hardened by the experience of brutal combat during World War 2, they decided to murder all the 'pure vors'.

This resulted in the so called Bitch Wars which lasted for decades. Due to a large number of 'suki', most gulags were divided into two separate zones: one for 'suki' and one for 'vors'.

After the breakup of the Soviet Union in the 1990s, the vory assumed a leading role within the Russian criminal hierarchy . The group was able to "infiltrate the top political and economic strata while taking command of the burgeoning crime network that spread murderously through the post-Soviet countries."

Thieves In Law are given the title by other vory and in order to be accepted they must demonstrate considerable leadership skills, personal ability, intellect, charisma as well as a well-documented criminal history. Once accepted they must live according to the thieves' code. The penalty for violation of this code is often mutilation or death. Reportedly, "today the Vory have spread around the world, to Madrid, Berlin, and New York" and are "involved in everything from petty theft to billion-dollar money-laundering while also acting as arbiters among conflicting Russian criminal factions."

Reportedly, as capitalism began to take hold in Russia, an increasing number of college educated criminals began to take over more lucrative ventures. While these new criminal elements first worked with the Vory in the 1990s, in the first decade of the 21st century, ties to big business and government grew in importance. Consequently, while the "Vory are still strong in gambling and retail trade," their importance in Russian economy and society has decreased. However since the majority of criminals eventually are arrested and incarcerated, at some point they will come in contact with the Vory who are at the top of the hierarchy of the criminal world within the penal system in Russia.

One famous Vor V Zakone is Vladimir Podatev who was appointed a member of the commission for human rights under President Boris Yeltsin, in spite of three previous felony convictions for murder, assault, and rape. Another famous vor is Vyacheslav Ivankov, notorious mobster with convictions in both the former Soviet Union and the United States who was assassinated in 2009.

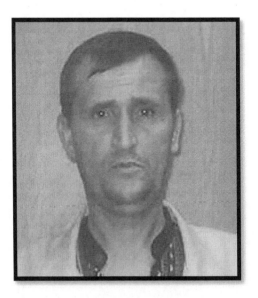

The Thief's Code

Vors consider prisons their true home and have a saying 'The home for angels is heaven and the home for a Vor is prison.' According to Aleksandr Gurov, an expert on the Vory who headed the organized crime units of the Soviet Interior Ministry and the GRU, "unlike the Cosa Nostra the Vory have 'less rules, but more severe rules' [and the] members must have no ties to the government, meaning they cannot serve in the army or cooperate with officials while in prison. They must also have served several jail sentences before they can be considered. They also are not allowed to get married."

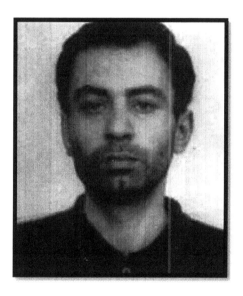

Furthermore, according to Michael Schwirtz, "ethnicity has rarely determined whether someone can join the club, and today many members, even those active inside Russia, are from other post-Soviet countries such as Armenia, Ukraine, Georgia, or Chechnya, and are not ethnic Russians."

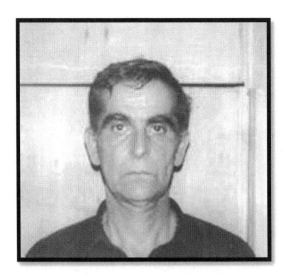

Under the theoretical code of the vory, a thief must:

Not have emotions

Forsake his relatives: father, mother, brothers, sisters.

Not have a family of his own: no marriage, no children; this does not however, preclude him from having an unlimited number of women. *During a large gathering of thieves-in-law during the late 1980s, this rule was removed.

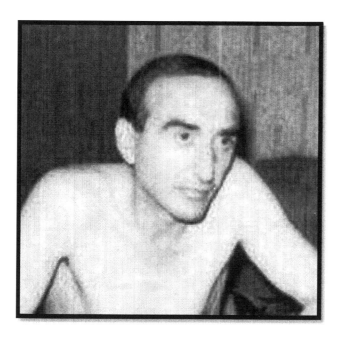

Never, under any circumstances, have a legitimate job or significant property (i.e. a house), no matter how much difficulty this brings; live only on money obtained through gambling or theft (the word 'theft' as used here describes any criminal activity considered 'legitimate' by the Vory), and rely on lower-level criminals for accommodation.

For example, harming or molesting children is strongly frowned upon and may endanger a vor's status and could provoke a more brutal retaliation from one's comrades than from the police. A 'thief in law' is a leadership position, so direct participation in arms smuggling and drug trafficking is incompatible with their high status since those crimes are a form of commerce. However receiving tribute from smugglers and drug-dealers or robbing and extorting them is a legitimate activity for a 'thief in law'.

Help other thieves: both by moral and material support, utilizing the commune of thieves.

Rule and arbitrate the criminal world and protect basic needs of criminals' and prisoners according to the extents and priorities set by the thieves' commune (typically in a given prison/prison cell) or region when not imprisoned)

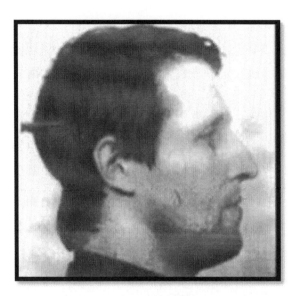

Keep secret information about the whereabouts of accomplices (i.e. dens, districts, hideouts, safe apartments, etc.).

In unavoidable situations (if a thief is under investigation or is arrested) to take the blame for someone else's crime; this buys the other person time to escape and remain free.

Demand an inquiry and judgment by a council of thieves to resolve disputes in the event of a conflict between oneself and other thieves, or between thieves.

If necessary, participate in such inquiries if called upon.

Punish any offending thief as decided by the judgment of the thieves' council

Not resist carrying out the decision of punishing the offending thief who is found guilty, with punishment determined by the thieves' council.

Have good command of the thieves' slang (called "Fenya"), a distinct language spoken by hardcore criminals in Russia and understood by few outsiders.

Never gamble without being able to cover losses.

Be good at playing card games for money.

Teach the criminal way of life to youth with potential.

Have, if possible, informants from the rank and file of thieves.

Not to lose your reasoning abilities when drunk.

Have nothing to do with the authorities (particularly with the ITU, Correctional Labor Authority), not participate in public activities, nor join any community organizations.

Not serve in the military or accept any weapons from the government or prison authority (police baton).

Make good on promises given to other thieves.

 Never deny his Vor status directly. To the questions like 'Are you a Vor?' or 'Who are you for life?', Vor should always answer: "Yes (Vor)", even if it is asked by police and videotaped. The latter question phrase is ritual and video footage containing the answer is commonly used by the Russian police to illustrate vors arrests in the media.

The above code is no longer in use besides the standard prison code of ethics of not cooperating with prison authorities or informing on your fellow inmates. Aleksandr Solzhenitsyn, author of The Gulag Archipelago, claimed never to have seen any thief honor the code if it conflicted with his personal criminal wants.

Tattoos

The Vory subculture (more exactly: the prison inmate subculture where Vory are the respectful leaders) are well known for having very well-made tattoos.

The tattoos are usually done in the prison with primitive tools.

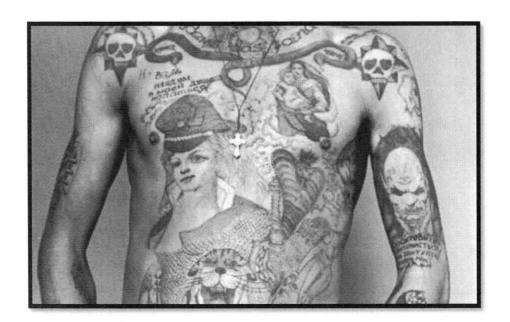

Many tattoos have special meanings, like "I've lost my freedom due to woman", "murderer" or "prison-born" (a tattoo of a baby).

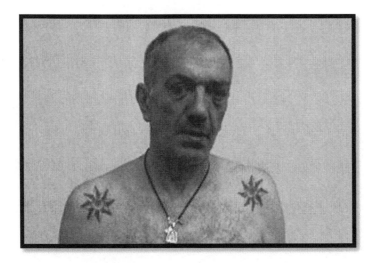

Some tattoos, like large Christian crosses, a Russian Orthodox cathedral with onion-shape cupolas, or military rank insignia tattoo on the shoulders, mean the Vor himself - the respected leader was "crowned" (approved) during a Vory meeting.

Female prison inmates also often have tattoos, like "they are tired" on the feet.

In the USSR, it was a well-known fact that the ordinary person must never have a tattoo which denotes a Vor, and, if the criminals will see such a person, he will be "asked" (offended, sometimes deadly) by them for being an impostor of a Vor.

According to some ex-law-enforcement officers like Dmitry Puchkov, this gradually ceased with the USSR downfall.

"Ponyatiya" (literally "the notions") is the rules of conduct (or even the customary law or code of honor) among prison inmates, with Vory being respectful leaders and judges according to these rules.

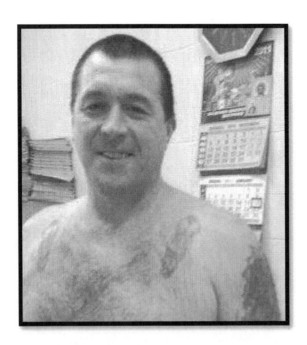

The "vorovskie ponyatiya" - the requirements for aspiring Vors, are listed above. However, there are also "ludskie ponyatiya" - requirements for all prison inmates ("ludi" - "people", in this meaning more like proletariat).

(A "Thief family)

The important part of "ludskie ponyatiya" is that everybody is required to maintain his own honor, mainly by avoiding doing any impure, humiliating and thus taboo. Examples are cunnilingus (or even telling detailed accounts of your sexual exploits) or picking up items from the floor - are collectively named "zapadlo".

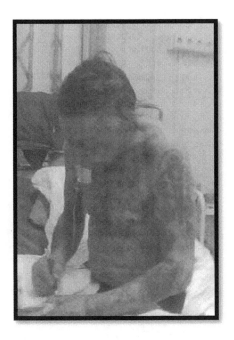

Touching a "petukh" ("rooster"), or accepting items from his hands, is also forbidden. More so, the floor is considered to be impure not due to hygienic reasons, but because the "roosters" touch the floor when they walk.

Also, "ponyatiya" prohibit the use of terms used in the Criminal Code and Criminal Procedure Code. For instance, one must not say "witness" ("svidetel'"), one must say "ochevidetz" ("beholder").

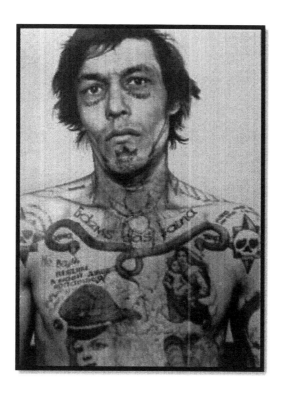

Some words like "to ask from someone" are taboo because they denote 'payment' for doing, or saying something that violates ponyatiya. This 'payment' occurs when one offends another due to violating "ponyatiya", such as dishonesty in monetary affairs. Due to the deadly nature of this sort of conflict; asking questions must be in the form of "he was interested", not "he asked me".

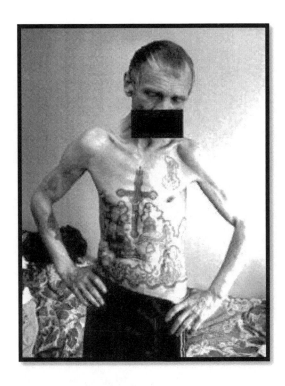

 Some words are considered to be deadly verbal insults, often punishable by murder - like "rooster" (more so - anything related to bird and feather), "kozel" ("goat") and so on.

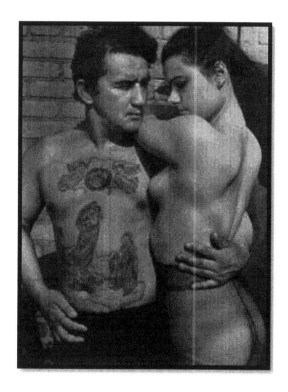

According to "ponyatiya", women are disrespected and considered to be equal to animals. Thus, the opinion of the women can never be significant. A man who betrays his male friends due to a romantic affair is despised.

"Petukhi" ("the roosters")

These are the lowest layer of inmates, something like the pariahs. They are the subject of constant humiliating acts (including anal rape) from other inmates.

They are not allowed to touch the "normal" inmates or to share any items with them, and occupy the worst places in the prison cell. Contacting a "petukh" is "zapadlo" and can sometimes even lead the other person to be declared a "petuh" - usually by beating and knocking under the bed ("pod shkonku").

Sometimes, a person can become a "petukh" due to the offense for which he is imprisoned. Sexual offenses, especially against minors or women completely unknown to the offender (street rapes), are an example (rape of women after being her guest and drinking with her is not considered a humiliating deed). Homosexual acts were illegal from 1933 to 1993, and all those jailed for this were automatically considered petukhi.

The status of "petukh" is lifelong and cannot be cancelled. A "petukh" is obliged to warn everybody on his status (the standard formula - "I have problems in this life") in any new prison/camp he is relocated, and even in his possible next imprisonment after serving the current punishment and liberation. Otherwise, it is considered that he polluted ("zashkvaril") the normal people who communicated to him being unaware of his "petukh" status, this can cause severe beating or even a murder.

IN THEIR OWN WORDS

Ya nechevo ne znayu: **Russian for "I don't know anything. I didn't see anything"**

"The Russians (Gangsters) didn't come here to enjoy the American dream. They came here to steal it." **New York State tax agent Roger Berger**

"What if they refused to pay? We'd beat them in their store right in front of everybody. But they paid. They knew what was coming if they didn't pay. They knew they'd get murdered, if they don't pay." **A Brighton Beach New York gangster who worked for Russian mobster Evsei Argon. Argon himself once threatened to kill a Russian émigré's daughter on her wedding day if he didn't pay $15,000.**

"Do you know who shot you?"
"Yes,"
"Who? We'll take care of it"
"I'll take care of it myself."
Conversation between Evsei Agron and a New York City Police Detective in the hospital after Agron had been shot in the belly

Emile Puzyretsky: "You have to pay! Otherwise, you're not going to live! And if you survive, you're not going to be able to work anymore!"
Merchant: Willy, please don't terrorize me anymore," "We aren't livin' in a jungle. We live in U.S.A."
Emile Puzyretsky "You fuckin' rat... I'll make you a heart attack. This is the last time you'll be able to see. If you don't give the money . . . just wait and see what's goin' to happen to you."
Taped conversation between Brighton Beach gangster Emile Puzyretsky and a merchant who was being extorted for $50,000 on orders of mob boss Evsei Argon. The merchant paid, with interest.

"If (Evsei) Agron had been an honorable godfather, he wouldn't have had to use brute force to extort shopkeepers "Instead, he would have been showered with gifts, both as a sign of honor" **Resident of Brighton Beach**

"The Italians don't kill civilians—not even the family members of rats. The Russians have no such codes," **James DiPietro, a criminal attorney in Brooklyn who has represented both Russian and Italian underworld figures**

"The Russians wouldn't talk to us. They said, 'What can you do to us after the KGB and the Gulag?' The only thing they were afraid of is that we would deport them, and we won't do that. **Russian-speaking FBI agents discussing Russian-Jewish gangsters in Brighton Beach**

"I love my dad very much. My father's my world to me. There was a lot of harassment, a lot of fights. I just got very upset and I threw a book at his head. They [the school] made me see a psychologist." **Aksana Elson, daughter of Monya Elson in 1990 on why she assaulted a classmate**

"If you want trouble.....I'm ready" **Gangster Boris Goldberg, an Ex Israel army officer to gangster Evsei Agron during a "Sit down" a peace conference negotiation in May of 1984. During the conference Agron**

threatened Goldberg who instructed Agron to look out the window. The parking lot was filled with Goldberg's men, each carrying a rifle.
.

"I knew when I got out of jail that Biba [Boris Nayfeld's nickname] would still be in the ballpark. He would be a fucking problem," Elson said derisively. "Everybody said Biba, Biba. Biba Shmeeba. I said he was a piece of ass. He's a fucking nobody. And somebody sent word to Biba that I'm cursing him. And I said yes, I want to meet the motherfucker. He was a piece of shit] For this reason, I declared the war! I said, he cannot be what he wants to be! He's a mussor (A rat) in his heart. He wanted to be somebody. He was never nobody. You know, to be a godfather you have to have leadership qualities. He don't have any qualities." **Gangster Monya Elson, who left Israel to resettle in Brooklyn, on his rival Boris Nayfeld.**

"They were like two gunslingers who had to prove themselves top gun." **DEA official on the feud between Jewish mobsters Boris Nayfeld and Monya Elson**

"I never felt anti-Semitism but I used that as an excuse when I applied for my visa" [to the US in 1977]. **Russian gangster Marat Balagula**

"I love this country. It's so easy to steal here!" **Ludwig Fainberg on the United States.**

"America's built on Mafia! All over the world, when you ask 'What do you know about America?' they say, 'Mafia, "Godfather," Bugsy Siegel, Meyer Lansky!' I swear I can't believe John Gotti got life in jail. How can you kill your own history?" **Ludwig Fainberg**

"Tarzan was a boisterous, bigmouthed yiddel. He's a Jew boy, you know. Just a bigmouthed kid, always bragging, boisterous — but very nice, very kind." **Miami gangster speaking with affection for Tarzan AKA Ludwig Fainberg**

"Look, that's what they can offer. Life is a business. It's a trade. You want to give something for nothing? You can help once or twice. But then ten, twenty or forty times? For that you want to get something in return." **Ludwig Fainberg to undercover journalist's question "You don't have a problem with pushing women who are absolutely destitute into prostitution?"**

"You can buy a woman for $10,000 and you can make your money back in a week if she is pretty and she is young. Then everything else is profit." **Ludwig**

Fainberg to undercover journalist

"I think 10 percent don't know what they're getting into. Ninety percent know exactly what they're going to do. What they may not know exactly is the conditions or how much money they will get." **Ludwig Fainberg on the prostitutes he imported from Eastern Europe**

"My opinion is a prostitute is someone who is selling herself. From that point of view, that is what they are. It is true they definitely do not want to do this. They are being pushed by their social level of their life. They're getting pushed by necessity. They're being pushed to survive. Then maybe they're not really prostitutes." **Ludwig Fainberg**

"The girls come here and they send some money home and the family lives. If they don't come to work here or in Germany or England, their family suffers. I give the girls a chance to earn money. For me, it is a business transaction, plain and simple, but I am also helping these women out." **Ludwig Fainberg**

"That is bullshit. I never trafficked in women. I don't need trafficked women. Agents in Russia are overwhelmed with women who want to do this voluntarily. If you look at their living conditions in Russia, there is no way of surviving. They live in poverty. At least this way, they can make a living. When people need to eat, what are you going to do?" **Ludwig Fainberg to the charge by the US Department of State that he was a White Slaver**

"Tarzan (Ludwig Fainberg) doesn't care about anyone except himself. He has no loyalty to anyone. One night he cut the commissions the girls get on drinks. They went ballistic. I said, 'Wait till the end of the shift. They are threatening to go on strike.' He backed off. I said, 'Why do you always have to screw everything up?' He was a piece of shit!" **Ludwig Fainberg AKA Tarzan's former bodyguard**

"Poland wasn't an obvious transshipment point for drugs. It's not Bogota or Bangkok. They shot gunned each plane with three, four, or five couriers, all unknown to each other. They moved eight to ten kilos per flight, and it went on a good year before we caught on to it." DEA agent on the narcotics routes developed by Brooklyn gangster **Boris Nayfeld. In Manhattan, the dope was out of S&S Hot Bagel Shop, next to Katz's Delicatessen on East Houston Street in Manhattan.**

"I never lost consciousness. I wanted to shoot this guy. You can't imagine how hot and painful the wound was. But I saw the guy, a black man, run away. I was going to shoot him. I didn't have the strength to shoot him. The bullets made two holes in my stomach. My liver was severed. My pancreas was shattered. One bullet lodged in my left kidney and exploded." Doctors removed the kidney, along with twenty feet of intestine. "If I had gotten there twenty seconds later, I would have been on a slab. They put me on a stretcher and I lost consciousness. There was a lot of puss in my pancreas, which was abscessed. There was a lot of puss in my stomach. And the doctors said to my wife: 'He's going to die now.' And they put a tube into my heart. I heard 'morgue,' somehow I reacted. I twitched my toe as if to say I'm alive. They put me back in ICU. Then I had an operation. They told my wife I had a fifty-fifty chance; if I survived the first forty-eight hours, I might live. ... I spent twenty-eight days in intensive care; my wife was advised to say her farewell to me." **Monya Elson on his attempt assassination plotted by his rival in Brighton Beach,** Boris **Nayfeld.**

"If he doesn't like one word that comes out of your mouth, you're dead," **American hoodlum who worked with Russian gangster Monya Elson**

"I said, 'Hey Monya, you can't kill people for that.' He said, 'Yes I can! '" **American hoodlum who worked with Russian gangster Monya Elson**

"They would just go into places in Brooklyn and make them pay $25,000 a clip for protection, or else they'd use a ball peen hammer on them. The Russians are scared to death of the Italians. They scored over half a million dollars by shaking these guys down." **New York City Police Detective on how the Mafia, particularly Colombo Family operative Frankie "the Bug" Sciortino, (Born 1933) had been extorting money from Brighton Beach gangsters in the early years of the 1980s.**

"He said I was a musor. (An informant) I wanted to kill him. He thought that because I was a Jewish guy, and I had presumably left Russia forever, that it would be okay to play with Monya. Half the criminals will think I killed for revenge. The other half will think that maybe he knew something, and I killed [him] to shut his mouth. Revenge is the sweetest form of passion!" **Monya Elson on why he murdered a Russian gangster after his release from an Israeli prison in 1990.**

"Can you imagine if the gun went off? My brains would have been scrambled eggs." Monya **Elson on the failed assassination attempt against him. The assassin had the pistol pointed to the back his neck, pulled the trigger, but the gun jammed.**

"He started crying, the big motherfucker, and admitted that Nayfeld had paid him to kill me," He asked for forgiveness. We are not in the church. He was huge, big, and mean. He was a monster, a cold-blooded killer. The FBI has to give me an award." **Monya Elson the 1985 murder of Alexander Slepinin, AKA The Colonel, a three-hundred-pound, six-foot-five-inch killer paid by Boris Nayfeld to kill Elson. Slepinin was a former member of the Russian Special Forces, who had served in Afghanistan during the war against the Mujahedeen. He had tattoos of a panther and a dragon on his upper torso, meaning he had also been in a Gulag. He was an expert in martial arts, and kept a collection of swords and knives, which he used to dismember his victims in his bathtub before disposing of the body parts. He carried a business card that said he specialized in the techniques of mortal combat.**

"The shnook couldn't figure out how to wire the bomb. The device exploded in the man's hands, blowing them off." **LA Police Detective on a failed attempt to place bomb under Monya Elson's car**

"...nobody was hurt. It was wintertime, and Ukleba ran out of the rubble in his underwear. He ran all the way to Austria," **Monya Elston on the attempt to kill Brooklyn gangster Shlava Ukleba while he was visiting Moscow. The bomb planted in Ukleba's hotel destroyed a total of five room but left Ukleba untouched.**

"We're not saints. We Italians will kill you. But that's that. The Russians are crazy -- they'll kill your whole family." **Member of the Gambino Crime Family**

"They'll shoot you just to see if their gun works." **Brooklyn New York Detective on the Russian Mafia.**

"Marat was the king of Brighton Beach. He had a Robin Hood complex. People would come over from Russia and he'd give them jobs. He liked professional men. Guys came over and couldn't practice medicine or use their engineering degrees. He sought them out. He was fascinated with intellectuals. He co-opted them. He put them into the gasoline business; he put them into car washes or taxi companies. He'd reinvest his own money in their business if they were having trouble. He had a heart." **A former gangster from Brighton Beach**

"Everybody in Brighton Beach talked about Balagula in hushed tones. These were people who knew him from the Old Country. They were really, genuinely scared of this guy." **Suffolk County, New York, Prosecutor**

"Elson had very capable guys that he brought in as reinforcements from Israel and the former Soviet Union. But every week, one of them would get their heads blown off by a shotgun blast. Even Monya realized it was time to get out." **Brighton Beach Gangster**

"The Hamptons are filling up with Russians," Mike Morrison, a criminal investigator with the IRS told me. "When we ask them where they got the money to purchase their house or business, they produce a document from Uncle Vanya in St. Petersburg who says it's a gift. There is nothing we can do." **IRS Agent**

"If you cut off the head, and the arms and feet are missing, too, you can't get a positive identification on the torso. It's brilliant," **Homicide Detective on the Russians habit of hacking their victims apart.**

"It was a nice scam until it got into the hands of the Russians. They bought Rolls and Ferraris and walked around Atlantic City with stacks of hundred-dollar bills, and suddenly the IRS realized they were getting fucked for hundreds of millions of dollars." **An underworld attorney, in 1985 on what was then the relatively new scam of collecting gasoline tax at the pump and pocketing it.**

"If a bill was $1,500, the tip would be $1,500. If a guy would come over and sing a song, Marat would give him a hundred-dollar bill. I remember saying to myself, 'These people need intensive psychiatric help.'" **A Genovese gangster on Marat Balagula**

"Marat says he's got a photographic memory, but he don't. (**Gambling at the tables in Atlantic City**) We lost $20,000. I told Marat, 'How the fuck do you remember anything?'" **A Genovese gangster on Marat Balagula**

"I hate to be the bearer of bad tidings, but the FBI has reliable information that a major Russian organized crime figure has taken out a contract on your life." **NYC Editor to investigative reporter Robert I. Friedman who wrote regularly about the Russian Mob in America**

"Friedman! You are a dirty fucking American prostitute and liar! I WILL FUCK YOU! And make you suck my Russian DICK!" **Threat to reporter Friedman sent in a Hallmark Valentine Day's card that read "It was easy finding a Valentine for someone like you.". It was signed by the sender, Vyacheslav Kirillovich Ivankov. He later mailed a second threat that he included his cell block unit and prison ID number.**

"The Russians are ruthless and crazy. It's a bad combination. They'll shoot you just to see if their gun works." **NYC cop**

"Hell, it took them about a week to figure out how to counterfeit the $100 Super Note," **A senior Treasury Department official on Russian mobsters. The $100 super note was unveiled in 1997 with much fanfare as tamper-proof.**

"The Russians didn't come here to enjoy the American dream. They came here to steal it." **New York State tax agent Roger Berger**

"It's wonderful that the Iron Curtain is gone, but it was a shield for the West. Now we've opened the gates, and this is very dangerous for the world. America is getting Russian criminals. Nobody will have the resources to stop them. You people in the West don't know our Mafiya yet. You will, you will!" **Boris Urov, the former chief investigator of major crimes for the Russian attorney general.**

"Nobody remembers the first man who walked on the moon. Everybody remembers Al Capone." **Monya Elson**

"For Russians, enough is never enough. If a Russian makes $20 million, he wants $40 million. They never know when to stop. There is a saying in Russia: 'The house is burning and the clock is ticking.' It means you have to keep making money every minute. Even Russian racketeers and crooks want their children to be doctors and lawyers. But some of the kids have learned that they can make more money by being crooks. Young Russian kids with MBAs are getting jobs on Wall Street. They are setting up all kinds of scams. They'll hurt a lot of people. There'll be a lot of suicides. In this country, it's so easy to make money. I love this country. I would die for it." **Russian Gangster in Brighton Beach New York**

"You can't work a homicide in Brighton Beach. The Russians don't talk. Someone could get whacked in a club in front of a hundred diners, and nobody would see anything. So they will kill with impunity." **61st Precinct(Brighton Beach) Homicide Detective**

"Why are we being victimized by noncitizens who can run to Israel or Russia and can't be extradited? The Russian gangsters have told me that they've come here to suck our country dry. My uncle died on the beaches of Normandy defending this country. How did the Russian mob become so entrenched? They are into Social Security, Medicare, and Medicaid fraud. Why is it that every ambulance service in Brooklyn is run by the Russian mob? Why are so many of their doctors practicing without a license? They have invaded Wall Street from boiler-room operations to brokerage houses. Nothing is too small for them to steal. Even the guys with the multimillion-dollar Medicare scam still have to have their food stamps. The first generation are all thieves. Maybe the second generation will become a little more American." **NYC Police Officer**

Russian-American Mobsters

Berman, David: Las Vegas Casino Boss. FAKA Davie the Jew: Born 1903. Died 1957. Berman was born in Odessa, the Ukraine, the son of a former rabbinical student. Berman would remain steadfastly religious throughout his life, even helping Bugsy Seigel to fiancé the first synagogue in Las Vegas. (A four-bedroom house) When Berman was still a child, the family moved to South Dakota, as part of a Jewish resettlement program funded by Baron Maurice de Hirsch. From there the Berman's moved to Iowa.

By 1916, Berman was running his own gang in Sioux City and eventually moved to Minneapolis where he developed a working relationship with the New York based Genovese Crime family. Berman prospered with prohibition and gambling. Working with him, in those days and throughout his entire criminal career was his brother Chickie and Israel Alderman AKA Ice Pick Willie. Berman enlisted in the Canadian army in World War 2 (He was rejected by the US Army based on his felony record) and served in an elite reconnaissance ranger's outfit.

After the war, Minneapolis elected a young racket busting Hubert Humprey as mayor. Humprey effectively pushed Berman, now a wealthy man, out of the city and into the waiting arms of Meyer Lansky and Bugsy Seigel in Las Vegas. Reportedly, the Genovese family in New York, which had investment money with Seigel, insisted that Berman and his men, be included in Seigel's dealings in Vegas.

Before leaving Minnesota, Berman married a former dancer named Gladys Ewald, a German –American who converted to Judaism. She took her own life, at age 39, shortly after her husband's death, by an overdose of sleeping pills. Her daughter Susan believed that she was murdered for refusing to give up her late husband's shares in casinos.

It was Berman and his manager, Gus Greenbaum who walked into the Flamingo Hotel on June 21, 1947, only hours after Bugsy Siegel was shot dead and announced "We're taking over" (Contrary to film legend, Berman did not shout the news. Rather he spoke the words softly)

By the early 1950s, Berman, his brother and Ice Pick Willie Alderman were either owners or, or partner's in the Riveria and was involved with the Flamingo, the El Cortez and the El Dorado casinos. Berman died in 1957 after entering the hospital for a simple surgery. Susan Berman also believed her father's death was also under mysterious circumstances. Susan later wrote a book, *Easy Street*, about her father and growing up as what she termed "A Jewish Mafia princess in Las Vegas" Susan Berman was a troubled woman whom friends described as "smart, intense, and complex woman who challenged the boundaries of friendships and relationships. She was also the victim of many phobias, including crossing bridges, riding in elevators, and staying above the third floor in hotels; and at one point, she rashly attempted to kill herself." A gifted writer who was in and out of mental asylums throughout most of her adults life, she was murdered in her home Las Angeles on December 24, 2000.

Blumenfeld, Isadore. Minnesota Crime Boss. AKA as Kid Cann. AKA Issy. Born September 8, 1900, Rumnesk, Romania of Russian parents.. Immigrated to the US in 1902. Lived at 5900 Oakland Avenue and 4700 Circle Down, Golden Valley, North Tyrol Hills. The son of a furrier. Died June 21, 1981 Minnesota based mobster, raised in Near North Minnesota. There are several versions of how he got the nickname but it is most likely that he took it after Abe Cann, the prizefighter.

Poverty forced Cann out of grammar school and onto the streets first as a newspaper boy and then, gradually, into the Minneapolis red light district where he learned the basics of prostitution and narcotics sales. Prohibition, and the proximity of the Canadian border, made him rich. Cann and his brother Harry Bloom were soon partners with the Capone organization in Chicago in a whisky smuggling operation that expanded to five states. (Harry was called Bloom, because the family changed its name to what they felt was the less Jewish, Bloom. Harry went a step further and legally changed his name to Yiddy Bloom). Their bootlegging years were brief. They entered the business in about 1928 and left it in 1933.

On August 23, 1933, a federal grand jury in Oklahoma City, Oklahoma charged Cann and his business partner Barney Berman with playing a role in the infamous Charles Urschell kidnapping with haphazard gangster George 'Machine Gun' Kelly. (Who did not actually own a machine gun). The charges were dropped. If Cann played any role in the kidnapping, it was probably as a fence to 'wash' the ransom money. He was sentenced to one year in the Workhouse in 1934 for operating a still

The brothers were quick to expand their criminal empire across the Twin Cities to New Orleans and other places, (Cann was indicted in New Orleans but he refused to appear at trial. The charges were dropped.) largely because they were willing to dabble in drugs and prostitution, two areas where Minneapolis's Irish mob boss Tommy Banks refused to trade in. In 1956, Banks and Cann became the largest investor in the Twin Cities Rapid Transit Company.

Nor where they reluctant to use violence when they had too. In 1928, Cann, who was with the notorious criminal Verne Miller, was accused of shooting officer James Trepanier, crippling him for life. During the gun battle, which started over a disturbing the peace call, another officer shot Cann in right leg.

On September 6, 1934, Howard Guilford, another reporter looking into public corruption, was murdered when gangsters drove his car off of Pillsbury Avenue and almost decapitated him with a shotgun blast to the neck. He died instantly. In 1927, gangsters had done the same thing to him. He survived, but barely and spent the remainder of his life in poor health. Guilford was killed because he planned to run for mayor of Minneapolis.

Then, on December 9, 1935, Walter Liggett, the publisher and editor of Plain Talk Magazine was shot five in front of his wife and ten-year-old daughter Marda, in a drive by shooting outside of his apartment in Minneapolis. Liggett was a crusader who reported on dozens of connections between Minnesota politicians, especially the Governor, Floyd Olson and criminals. Liggett, who came from an old Minnesota family, had been an early backer of Olson until he realized how corrupt and power mad Olson was.

The politicians responded by having Liggett beaten in October of 1935 by Cann. Liggett had written extensively on Cann's use of political influence and on October 23, 1935, Cann and Abe 'Brownie" Bronstein first offered Liggett money and favors if he would stop reporting. When he refused, they beat him up and then had him arrested for assault. The beating was severe. One of Liggett's ears was also ripped off and a tooth was kicked out of his mouth. Cann also arranged for Liggett to be arrested for statutory rape of a 19-year-old girl. Cann was arrested after Liggett was killed but on Feburary 19, 1935, Cann was found not guilty of killing Liggett but few believed the truthfulness of the trial. It was widely assumed then and today, that Cann had fixed jury and the State investigators. Oddly, Governor Olson died the following year, at age 44, of a stomach aliment.

On January 22, 1945, Cann was suspected in the murder of another reporter named Arthur Kasherman. Like the others, he was killed in a drive by shooting. His last words were "Don't shoot, for God's sakes don't shoot". Unlike the others,

Kasherman had a reputation as a minor extortionist, using his publication as means to shake down dirty politicians and policemen.

The brothers ran their empire from the Flame Night Club on Nicollet Avenue (it was later called the Club Carnival) and in 1942 the federal government dubbed him 'The vice lord of the Midwest' although Cann seems not to have been completely sane. He sometimes took on the persona of a character named Dr. Ferguson, or Fergie, millionaire philanthropist and he insisted that people refer to him by that name and title.

In the early 1950s, it was learned that Cann was an investor in the Mafia's schemes to skim the Las Vegas casinos. How much he got and from which casinos, was never learned. In 1959, Cann was convicted of violating the Mann Act (Transporting a female across state lines for immoral purposes) The case was thrown out on appeal. The woman in question was a professional prostitute from Chicago. However, in 196, other charges of extortion and jury tampering followed and Cann was finally sent to federal prison.

After his release from prison in 1964, Cann and his wife (Lillian Lee. They were married on August 25, 1936 and were childless) moved to Miami beach where he was thought to partners with Meyer Lansky. Cann had invested in several of Lansky's casinos back in the 1940s and on Lansky's advice, they also owned land on Miami's waterfront that was leased to large, national hotel chains. Cann died in 1981 at age 80.

In 1939, Yiddy Bloom (Born January 28, 1911) who ran a liquor store, married Verna Kraemer. The couple had two children, who, as adults, changed their name back to Blumenfeld. Yiddy also invested in real estate including 19 Florida hotels, which, according to the Florida Attorney General in 1968, were secretly owned by Meyer Lansky who was controlling them on behalf of various Mafia bosses.

In 1978, Yiddy pled guilty in a stock manipulation conspiracy case involving a scam to manipulate the common stock belonging to the Magic Marker Corporation from $6.50 to $30 a share. His son Jerrold was also indicted.

It was rumored in the underworld that after Meyer Lansky's daughter spent money set aside to care for her disabled brother Buddy Lansky, that Yiddy Bloom paid all of Buddy's medical bills. Yiddy died on November 18, 1994

Hoff Max: Bootlegger. Born 1893. In South Philadelphia, a son of Russian-Jewish, immigrants. Died April 27, 1941 AKA Boo-Boo. The nickname originated in South Philadelphia. The family lived in a predominately-Irish section and when Hoff's mother would call her son, Max brother Lou, in Yiddish; it sounded like she was calling Boo-Boo. The name stuck on Max rather than his brother and for the next 15 years, Hoff was called "Little Boo-Boo" until it was shortened to simply Boo-Boo.

Hoff quite school and worked as a newsboy and, while still a teen opened a political club in Philadelphia's Fifth Ward. The club was actually a front for what would become a large gambling casino.

Prohibition made him rich. By 1920, when he was 27 years old, Hoff was a millionaire. His payroll to city hall was said to exceed $150,000 a month, with one police official on the books for $25,000 a month. He operated two first rate night clubs in Philadelphia, The Ship and The Piccadilly and grossed at least $5,000,000 a year from bootleg sales. He also dabbled importing good whisky from Europe, which he haply sold to New York buyers and ran a side business importing and selling machine guns to the underworld. His money laundering empire was thought to "wash" ten million dollars a month. (The equivalent of $100 million today)

Boo-Boo himself never drank, smoked or gambled. He was indicted several times but never convicted.

Sports made him even richer. By the late 1920s, Hoff was one of the biggest and most important sports promoters in the country and owned the largest stable of professional fighters in the world. In 1927, Hoff filed a suit against Light Heavyweight boxer Gene Tunney and his manager, Billy Gibson, claiming that he and Tunney had a signed agreement that Hoff would sponsor the match fight. Tunney had, in fact, signed the document, but signed it "Eugene Joseph Tunney". His real name was James Joseph Tunney. Hoff dropped the suit in 1931 but never changed his story, claiming that Tunney had cheated him.

By 1933, it was all over. Boo-Boo, as smart as he was, was too flashy for his own good. The IRS moved in and charged him with owing $12,000 back taxes. His houses were sold at auction and whatever cash he had slipped away to lawyers who kept him out of jail. The rest probably went to gangsters who extorted him.

At the end of his life, he ran a malted shop, the Village Barn, in West Philadelphia.

He died in his sleep, at age 48 on April 27, 1941 at his home at 4723 Larchwood Avenue. His wife found a fifty-tablet bottle of sleeping pills, of which only six remained, so it was long assumed that he had committed suicide. However, the bottle was six years old. Hoff had died of a heart attack.

Katzenberg Jacob: Narcotics dealer. AKA Yasha. Born 1888. Born in Russia, raised on the Lower East Side of New York. Short and round with poor eyesight, Katzenberg was a major narcotics peddler to the underworld during the 1930s. His customers included New York's Lucky Luciano, Waxey Gordon, Boston's Charlie Solomon, Nig Rosen and the Frank Nitti organization in Chicago. In court in 1939, the dope peddler told authorities that he supplied Johnny Torrio, once Chicago mob boss, with narcotics through a connection named Frank Zagarino. He also claimed that it was Torrio who was his main source of liquor supplies during the prohibition.

He is also reported to have had outlets in Detroit, Kansas City and Saint Louis. The League of Nations, the latter day United Nation's, dubbed him "an international menace" and estimated his dope ring to be worth at least $10 million dollars. Katzenberg had been a bootlegger but when repeal came, he turned to narcotics peddling.

On Feburary 25 of 1935, authorities discovered Katzenberg's opium processing plant at 2919 Seymour Avenue in the Bronx, operated in the home of a Dr. Pietro Quinto, (Born 1891) a chemist and former Captain in the Italian Calvary, after a small fire broke out in the building for reasons unknown. Firemen called police who seized 980 ounces of morphine from the property, which then sold for about $125 an ounce. (A Dominick Palmizio was also arrested)

Based on the evidence from the plant and other casework, the police were able to charge Katzenberg and others with a series of crime. In December of 1938 he sentenced to ten years in prison and fined $10,000, a huge amount at that time, after he pled guilty. Jacob Lvovsky (AKA Jack Goode) and his assistants Sam Cross, (Real name Sam Gross) and Ben Feldman. All three worked in Katzenberg's operation as financiers, were also arrested and sentenced to six years in prison for bribing a US Customs official named John McAdams to allow tons of dope into the US. Sammy Lee, Katzenberg's top man in the trade was found murdered on October 22, 1934, left in a gutter on West Sixteenth Street in new York.

The night before he was killed, Lee visited Katzenberg in prison where Katzenberg gave him a postdated check for an unspecified amount. Pietro Quinto, the operations chemist was sentenced to eight year in prison as well. Agents also confiscated $37,000 from his various bank accounts. Initially, Katzenberg fled arrest and was eventually deported from Greece back to the United States to serve his sentence. In custody to federal authorities, he agreed to become a states witness. He was released with time served and disappeared from public view.

Katzenberg Jasha: Narcotics financier in the 1930s. He underwrote narcotic shipments from Tientsing China on behalf of Lepke Buchalter and his partner Joe Lvovsky. Katzenberg, who was eventually jailed, underwrote enough dope in the United States in 1938 "To tend to the need of 10,000 addicts" the US government claimed. Since the drugs were smuggled into the port of New York at a rate estimated sufficient to supply the current needs of a fifth of the country's then addict population, the imports soon came to Buchalter attention and he cut himself in for a third of the profits. Katzenberg and his partners had no choice but to agree.

Shapiro Jacob "Gurrah" (May 5, 1899-June 9, 1947) was a New York mobster who, with his partner Louis "Lepke" Buchalter, controlled industrial labor racketeering in New York for two decades and established the Murder, Inc. organization.

Born in Odessa (Russian Empire) in 1899. While confined in hospital in Brooklyn he became friends with Joe Valachi and Jimmy "The Shiv" DeStefano (who got his nickname while confined in the hospital). Jack "Legs" Diamond was also there but kept his distance from the feared threesome. During this period, Shapiro encountered his future partner, Louis Buchalter; both boys were attempting to rob the same pushcart. Instead of fighting over the spoils, Shapiro and Buchalter agreed on a partnership. Buchalter served as the brains and Shapiro provided the muscle in an alliance that lasted for decades. Shapiro and Buchalter soon become acquainted with future mobsters Meyer Lansky and Charles "Lucky" Luciano, both of whom were protégés of mobster Arnold "The Brain" Rothstein. Encouraged by Rothstein, Shapiro and Buchalter entered the lucrative arena of New York labor racketeering working for Jacob "Little Augie" Orgen. Orgen had previously wrested control of this racket from Nathan "Kid Dropper" Kaplan in the decade-long labor slugger wars. The gangsters had infiltrated labor unions in the busy Garment District of Manhattan, assaulting and murdering the union leadership to gain control. The gangsters then instituted a system of kickbacks and skimming from union dues while at the same time extorting the garment manufacturers with the threat of strikes. After working for Orgen for a while, Shapiro and Buchalter started planning to take over his operations. Realizing that Shapiro and Buchalter posed a threat, Orgen allied himself with brothers Eddie and Jack "Legs" Diamond. Shapiro and Buchalter soon made their move. On October 15, 1927, Orgen and Jack Diamond were standing on the corner of Delancey and Norfolk Street in the Lower East Side. Two gunmen (thought to be Shapiro and Buchalter) drove up to the corner. One gunman got out of the car and started shooting while the driver began shooting from the inside the car. Orgen was killed instantly and Jack Diamond was severely wounded. With Orgen's death, Shapiro and Buchalter took over his labor racketing operation. The two partners soon began massive extortions of both labor unions and businesses as they created a massive criminal monopoly in the Garment District.

Shapiro and Buchalter soon formed the infamous Murder, Inc., an organization that performed contract murders for organized crime. Their client was the "National Crime Syndicate", a confederation of crime families created by Luciano and Lansky in 1929. The Syndicate was created to avoid the bloody gang wars of the 1920s by creating an organization with the power to mediate organized crime disputes and punish offenders. Murder, Inc. served as the enforcement arm for the Syndicate. With Buchalter leading Murder, Inc., Shapiro and Albert "Mad Hatter" Anastasia were his most trusted associates. One of its most dedicated members, Shapiro personally oversaw many contract murders and recruited promising gunmen for future membership. During the early 1930s, US Attorney Thomas E. Dewey started to prosecute organized crime members in New York City. The pressure created by Dewey was such that in 1935 mobster Dutch Schultz asked the National Crime Syndicate to approve Dewey's murder. Shapiro and Anastasia agreed with Schultz, but Buchalter and the rest of the Syndicate turned down his request. Killing a prosecutor went against mob tradition, the majority argued, and would only increase federal investigation into organized crime and possibly expose the Syndicate itself. In fact, the Syndicate was so fearful of Schultz's proposal that they later ordered Buchalter to murder Schultz. On October 23, 1935, Schultz and several associates were gunned down by Murder, Inc. gunmen in a restaurant in Newark, New Jersey. Shortly after Schultz's death, Shapiro and Buchalter became the focus of Dewey's investigations. In October, 1936, Shapiro and Buchalter were convicted under the terms of the Sherman Anti-Trust Act and were both sentenced to two years in Sing Sing Prison. After his conviction, Shapiro went into hiding for a year. However, he finally turned himself in to Federal Bureau of Investigation (FBI) agents on April 14, 1938 and was sent to prison. On May 5, 1944, Shapiro was convicted of conspiracy and extortion and sentenced to 15 years to life in prison. Months before his 1944 conviction, Shapiro allegedly smuggled a note to Buchalter, who was then on trial in New York for murder. The note simply read, "I told you so." On March 4, 1944, Buchalter was electrocuted in Sing Sing Prison in Ossining, New York. Until his death in prison from a heart attack in 1947, Shapiro remained convinced that had Dewey been killed, he and others would have remained free.

Shenker, Morris: Casino operator. Died August 10, 1989 at age 82. A Russian born Jew, who had survived, even prospered in the Las Vegas underworld. He arrived in St. Louis in 1922, at age 15, able to speak only a few words of English. Shenker worked his way through law school at Washington University and went into practice in 1932. He was one the world's leading fundraisers for Israel. Called the "foremost lawyer for the mob in the U.S.," by Life Magazine, Shenker was a defense attorney from St. Louis who represented Teamsters' President James R. Hoffa.

Although he represented leading Mafia killers in St. Louis, Shenker was active in Democratic politics and was appointed by St. Louis Mayor A. J. Cervantes to serve as chair of the St. Louis

Commission on Crime and Law Enforcement. Shenker was forced to resign amid allegations that money from a $20 million dollar federal grant to fight crime was going to "unauthorized persons and causes "on the commission.

In 1983, federal agents investigating the skim at the Dunes Hotel in Las Vegas, owned largely by Shenker, (The secret owner, or least the major stockholder, of the Dunes was said to be Ray Patriarca, boss of the Rhode Island Mafia) discovered a multimillion-dollar fraud perpetuated by Russian-American gangster Evsei Agron, Murray Wilson and allegedly by Shenker.

According to the Justice Department, Shenker had arranged for Agron and a dozen members of his crew to fly into Las Vegas on all-expense-paid junkets. He then insured that each of the hoods with Agron were given lines of credit of up to $50,000. However, instead of gambling the money, they turned the chips over to Wilson who cashed them in and Shenker never repaid the casino for the markers. Over a period of several months, the scam defrauded the Dunes of more than $1 million. The government believed that Shenker had masterminded the scheme. Shenker eventually managed to drive the once proud Dunes Casino into Chapter 11. Indicted for personal bankruptcy fraud in 1989, he died before the government could prosecute him.

Solomon Charles. Boston Bootlegger. AKA "King Solomon" AKA Boston Charlie. Born 1884 Died January 6, 1932. Boston's most important bootlegger, Solomon allegedly worked alongside Joe Kennedy, father of President John F. Kennedy, in the bootlegging business, although this appears to be more legend that fact. He was also heavily involved in narcotic, prostitution and gambling.

A Russian immigrant, Solomon was raised in the West End in a middle class environment, the family owned a neighborhood movie house, but by his teen years, he was already dabbling in prostitution and fencing stolen goods. Prohibition put Solomon on the criminal map. He was powerful enough in the underworld to attend the Atlantic City Crime Conference in 1927.

He was constantly under investigation but was rarely convicted. He served 13 months in Atlanta Federal Prison on a perjury charge related to a narcotics case and in 1921, he was tried for his role in a million dollar mail robbery, but was not convicted.

The Kings Cotton Club in Roxbury

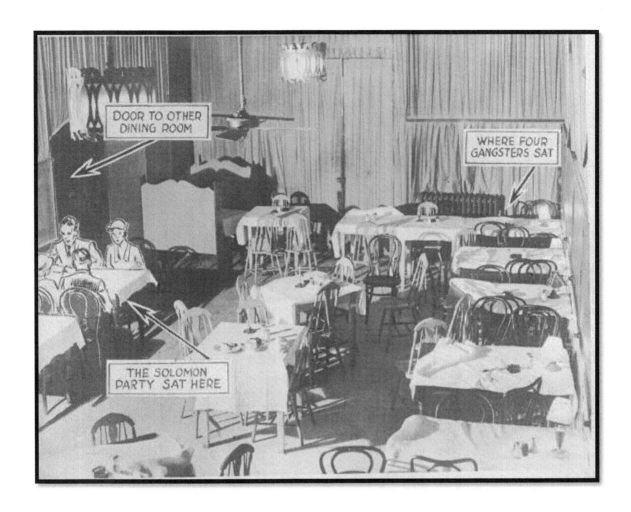

He was finally indicted in early in 1933, in New York federal court, with operating a liquor-smuggling ring. Federal prosecutors believed his underworld associates feared he would cooperate with investigators and decided to have him killed. They urged him to remain in custody awaiting trial, but he returned to the Boston area after posting $5,000 bail.

Solomon was assassinated in Boston on January 24, 1933. Four gunmen shot him in a men's room at the Cotton Club. Three bullets hit but Solomon managed to stagger out into the main dining hall but collapsed. An orchestra drowned out the noise of the shooting. About an hour before the shooting, Solomon had slipped

$5,000 from the cash register into his pocket. When police searched him in the hospital, all he had left on him was eighty cents and a check for $14.00 When asked who shot him, he answered "A dirty rat" William and Joe Ryan and Billy Brennan, local gangsters, were picked up for questioning in the case, but released.

Exactly who killed and why is not clear although it is largely agreed that Phil Buccola, who ran the Boston Mafia at the time, ordered Solomon's death in able to take over his rackets. When Solomon died, his once massive estate was valued at less than $4,000.

Lou Fox, right, in Chesterfield coat, leaves the courthouse in the early 1940's. Fox was an old Prohibition bootlegger, a protégé of King Solomon. Until his death of heart attack in 1963, "he ran the rackets in Revere out of his insurance office

Stacher Joseph: Gambler. AKA Doc Born 1902 Died 1977.

Born under the last name Oystacher in the Ukraine. Starcher arrived in the United States with his family in 1912 when he was ten years old. By the early

1920s, he was selling beer to distributors for Abner "Longy" Zwillman, in New Jersey. He was eventually promoted to manage Zwillman's extensive gambling operations in Northern New Jersey. In the 1930s, Stacher was working for Meyer Lansky in the West Coast and the Caribbean. When Las Vegas began to grow, Lansky moved Stacher to Nevada to oversee his interests there at the Sands and later at the Freemont Casinos. In the early 1960s, Stacher fell into Attorney General Bobby Kennedy's sites and was ordered deported to Poland. However Stacher used the Law of Return to move to Israel where he became a citizen in 1965. He died of a heart attack while on a trip to West Germany in 1977.

Made in the USA
Lexington, KY
12 August 2012